IAN FINDLEY
HEY, KIDS!

I0369274

This book is a collection of dad (Grandad) jokes, one sent every day by a Grandfather to his Grandkids for over two years.

It proved a great way to say, I think about you every day and you are never out of my mind.

It's a great way to say,

I love you, kids.

HEY, KIDS! We have got a new neighbour. He is Irish and a bit strange. He never goes into his house, he just stays outside all day.

His name is Patty,

Patty O'Furniture.

The writer of this book makes no claim of ownership or originality for the jokes it contains. The material in this book is simply a collection of jokes heard, read, been told and remembered over the years.
The jokes have been changed or adapted to suit a theme.

First published by Busybird Publishing 2023

Copyright © 2023 Ian Findley

ISBN: 978-1-922954-77-0

This book is copyright. Apart from any fair dealing for the purposes of study, research, criticism, review, or as otherwise permitted under the Copyright Act, no part may be reproduced by any process without written permission. Enquiries should be made through the publisher.

This is a work of fiction. Any similarities between places and characters are a coincidence.

Cover design: Busybird Publishing

Layout and typesetting: [insert name]

Busybird Publishing
2/118 Para Road
Montmorency, Victoria
Australia 3094
www.busybird.com.au

A daily joke for my Grandkids

"HEY, KIDS!"

Website: ifindbooks.com.au
Email: ifindbooks3@gmail.com

HEY, KIDS!
I read on the internet that humans eat more bananas than monkeys. I can believe that, I can't remember the last time I ate a monkey.

HEY, KIDS!
What do you call a person who eats another person very, very, slowly?

A Cannibble.

HEY, KIDS!
I just thought I would tell you about a new jumper I bought recently. It was giving off static electricity. It was shocking. I took it back to the store and they gave me another one free of charge.

HEY, KIDS!
A Priest, a Monk and a Rabbit walked into a blood bank.

The Rabbit said "I think I might be a typeO."

HEY, KIDS!
Which religious figure do chickens fear the most?

The Friar.

HEY, KIDS!
Someone asked me how to make a motherboard. I told him that I'd just talk to her about football.

HEY, KIDS!
The other day one of you asked me what procrastinate means? Just wait, I'll tell you later.

HEY, KIDS!
When your uncle was born, I wanted to call him Lance, but Grandma said no because it was too uncommon. I reminded her in medieval times people were called Lance a lot.

HEY, KIDS!
I went to the book store to see if they had any books on Turtles. The shop keeper said, hard back? I said yes, with little legs.

HEY, KIDS!
Years ago I went out with a girl who only had one leg. She worked in a Brewery. You won't believe it but she was in charge of the hops.

HEY, KIDS!
When I was building my first home, I asked the builder. how much it would cost to include a chimney?

He said nothing. It's on the house.

HEY, KIDS!
Why do French people eat a lot of snails?

Because they are not really into fast food.

HEY, KIDS!
The worst Pub I have ever been to is called The Fiddle. It was a vile Inn.

HEY, KIDS!
I once asked a Policeman how the hackers managed to escape?

He said, I think they just ransomware.

HEY, KIDS!
During Covid I got a new pair of gloves to match my mask. Unfortunately, both gloves were for the left hand. On one hand it's okay,
but on the other it's just not right.

HEY, KIDS!
Before the crowbar was invented did you know that most crows drank at home.

HEY, KIDS!
You've really got to hand it to you short people because they usually can't reach it for themselves.

HEY, KIDS!
What do I call a bulletproof Irishman?

Rick O'Shea.

HEY, KIDS!
Did you know that the umbrella was meant to be named the brella. It's just that the person who was naming it was a slow thinker and hesitated.

HEY, KIDS!
I'm done trying to be a people pleaser.
That is if everyone is okay with that.

HEY, KIDS!
Did you know that you can't use "beefsoup" as a password? Apparently, it's not stroganoff.

HEY, KIDS!
I've decided to build an elite army of babies.
I think I will call them the infantry.

HEY, KIDS!
What sport can a person who has lost
75% of their spine play?

American football. They can play as a quarterback.

HEY, KIDS!
I have developed this terrible condition where I just
can't stop making up jokes about airports.

My doctor says it's terminal.

HEY, KIDS!
When I was working, I can remember my boss coming
up to me and saying. "Where have you been,
I've been trying to find you all day?"

I reminded him, "Good employees are hard to find. "

HEY, KIDS!
Many people today are just too judgemental.
I can tell by just looking at their face.

HEY, KIDS!
I always knock on the fridge door before I open it just
in case there is a salad dressing.

HEY, KIDS!
I would like to have a space party but I'm not sure what
to do. I suppose I will need to planet.

HEY, KIDS!
I decided to take an airline company to court
after my luggage went missing.

I lost the case.

HEY, KIDS!
I decided to appeal the court decision with the airline. So, I went back with a ladder. I needed to take my case to a higher court.

HEY, KIDS!
What did the teacher at the Kamikaze School for Pilots say to his students?

Watch carefully I am only going to do this once.

HEY, KIDS!
I called an electrician to come and do a job at my house.

He refused.

HEY, KIDS!
There is a new strain of head lice going around that is resistant to all treatments.

This has left the doctors scratching their heads.

HEY, KIDS!
What did Yoda say when he saw himself on a 4K TV?

HDMI.

HEY, KIDS!
What did 50 do when he got hungry?

58.

HEY, KIDS!
I got mugged by 6 dwarfs yesterday on my walk.

Not Happy.

HEY, KIDS!
Grandma called out to me from the other room and asked, "do you ever get a sharp shooting voodoo type pain stabbing right through your entire body"?
I said no.

She said, "how about now"?

HEY, KIDS!
Grandma and I can never agree on vacations. I want to go to a relaxing island with 5 star accommodation. And, she always wants to come with me.

HEY, KIDS!
My Counsellor told me that I am totally incapable of expressing my feelings.

I can't say I'm surprised.

HEY, KIDS!
Now that I have got older, I don't like to look at myself and see a dad bod.

I prefer to see myself as a father figure.

HEY, KIDS!
What do you call a Cappuccino with a cold? Coughee.

HEY, KIDS!
What did the drummer name his twin daughters?

Anna 1 Anna 2.

HEY, KIDS!
My neighbour couldn't pay his water bill.
So, I sent him a "Get Well Soon" card.

HEY, KIDS!
Do you know why women are looking more beautiful during Covid? It's the mask era.

HEY, KIDS!
I heard your Grandma yelling at the TV. She was yelling "Don't go in there, don't go into the church you idiot." When I went to see what she was watching it was our wedding video.

HEY, KIDS!
I just dropped my phone in the pool.

Now it's syncing.

HEY, KIDS!
Grandma and I went out for dinner the other night and the waiter said "I can see that your glass is empty Sir, would you like another one?"

I replied no. Why would I want 2 empty glasses?

HEY, KIDS!
My doctor just told me that I am going deaf.
This was hard for me to hear.

HEY, KIDS!
Most people are shocked when they find out that I am not a very good electrician.

HEY, KIDS!
The Police told me to prepare myself for the worst regarding Grandma's disappearance. So, I went back to the op shop and got her clothes back.

HEY, KIDS!
I'm sending out a big thank you to the person who played triangle in your school orchestra.

Thank you for every ting.

HEY, KIDS!
You won't believe it but I have been offered a job teaching poetry in a prison. I spent all last night thinking about the pros and cons.

HEY, KIDS!
I accidentally deleted an audio book that Grandma and I were listening to. Now I will never hear the end of it.

HEY, KIDS!
Anyone want to buy a broken barometer?
There's no pressure.

HEY, KIDS!
I never wanted to believe that Grandma was stealing from her job as a traffic controller. But when I got home all the signs were there.

HEY, KIDS!
I now clean all my weapons with tree sap. Some say I am crazy but I'm sticking to my guns.

HEY, KIDS!
Did you know that there's a band called 999MB.

They haven't had a gig yet.

HEY, KIDS!
Have you heard about the girl who only eats plants?

I wouldn't be surprised if you haven't
heard of herbivore.

HEY, KIDS!
Are you ever surprised how little people
change? Actually, the process is the same as big
people its just that they have smaller clothes.

HEY, KIDS!
I just found out that my new neighbour is a ghost.
I had my suspicions the moment he walked
through the door.

HEY, KIDS!
I did some cooking yesterday. Unfortunately, I burnt my
Hawaiian Pizza. Now I know that I should have cooked
it on Aloha temperature.

HEY, KIDS!
During the Covid lockdown I got out a map of the
world, put it on the wall and asked Grandma to throw a
dart at it. I told her that wherever it lands I will take her
there when the Covid lockdown ends. It looks like our
next holiday is going to be behind our fridge.

HEY, KIDS!
When your mother handed me my 70th birthday card
this year I looked at her and said,
"one would have been enough".

HEY, KIDS!
Why can't you call someone a sick eagle?

Because it's illegal.

HEY, KIDS!
The first rule of the Passive Aggression Club is:

You know what, never mind, it's fine.

HEY, KIDS!
I decided to release my own fragrance.

Unfortunately, the people on the bus were not impressed.

HEY, KIDS!
The cow wasn't thinking too much about the upcoming visit of the butcher, mainly because she had an udder problem to worry about.

HEY, KIDS!
I developed a fear of speed bumps but I'm slowly getting over it.

HEY, KIDS!
What's the difference between a dog and a Marine Biologist?

One wags his tail and the other tags his whale.

HEY, KIDS!
How can you tell the sex of an ant?

Put it in water. If it sinks it's a girl ant, if it floats its boy - ant.

HEY, KIDS!
I have invented a car that will only go when the driver is silent.

It goes without saying.

HEY, KIDS!
People have said that I wouldn't be any good at poetry because I am dyslexic.

But they were wrong. So far, I have made 3 pots and a vase and they are lovely.

HEY, KIDS!
Grandma can be really mean sometimes. She told me that I am not allowed to impersonate a flamingo anymore. Enough is enough and I had to put my foot down.

HEY, KIDS!
What do you call a magician who has lost his magic. Ian.

HEY, KIDS!
My friend Harold once told me that he hoped that I would die in a big hole filled with water. I know he meant "well".

HEY, KIDS!
A poem for you to ponder
I dig, you dig,

He digs, she digs,

We dig, they dig,

In the end we all dig.

It's not very long but it's deep.

HEY, KIDS!
When I was little my mother would feed me alphabet soup and tell everyone that I loved it. She was really just putting words in my mouth.

HEY, KIDS!
They have just dug up a Mummy in Egypt and discovered that it was buried in chocolate.

They think it is Pharoah Roche.

HEY, KIDS!
Grandma has not been feeling well so I am sending her to the doctor to get a referral to an archaeologist.

HEY, KIDS!
I just got in my car, put it in reverse and thought to myself. This takes me back.

HEY, KIDS!
Everyone has heard of the historical figure Karl Marx. But very few people have heard about his sister Onya. She invented the starting pistol.

HEY, KIDS!
I can remember going to a job interview and being told that the starting salary would be around $60,000 a year. But, they said, later that will become $80,000. Okay, I told them, I'll come back later.

HEY, KIDS!
What is the opposite of a croissant?

A happy Uncle. Ha Ha.

HEY, KIDS!
What type are music do Windmills like?

They are really big metal fans.

HEY, KIDS!
I have decided to put everything I own into an experimental program for feeding cattle cannabis. You know the steaks have never been higher.

HEY, KIDS!
Someone broke into my house and stole all my lamps.

I really should be upset but actually I am just delighted.

HEY, KIDS!
Grandma said that she would like me to treat her the way I did before we got married. So, I took her to a movie, out to dinner and dropped her off at her parents' place.

HEY, KIDS!
I employed an exorcist to perform an exorcism on my house. Unfortunately, I forgot to pay the bill. Now it's been repossessed.

HEY, KIDS!
Why can't skeletons play church music?

Because they don't have any organs.

HEY, KIDS!
I wasn't originally going to get a brain transplant but then I changed my mind.

HEY, KIDS!
I decided to collect honey and start my own bee hive. I went to an Apiary and purchased my first two bees. When I got home, I discovered that there were three bees in the little matchbox that was provided. I immediately rang the man at the Apiary to point out his mistake. He told me not to worry the third one was a freebie.

HEY, KIDS!
Did you hear about the cannibalistic lion.

He swallowed his pride.

HEY, KIDS!
I dropped a tub of margarine on my foot about 3 weeks ago and it's still very sore.

I can't believe it's not better.

HEY, KIDS!
A bear walks into a bar and says "I'll have a gin and........ and .... and .... and .... and .... tonic". Okay says the Bartender but why the big pause?

The Bear looks down and says "I don't know I guess I was born with them".

HEY, KIDS!
Before I met your Grandma, I had a girlfriend who was obsessed with horoscopes. In the end, it Taurus apart.

HEY, KIDS!
What did the astronaut Buzz Aldrin, the second man to step onto the moon, say to the press when he returned to earth?

"Neil before me".

HEY, KIDS!
I just bought a new sword. It doesn't weigh much.

It's my light sabre.

HEY, KIDS!
I was looking in the cupboard and found the suitcases we used last year for our retirement trip.
I told them there will be no trips this year.

Now I have to deal with emotional baggage.

HEY, KIDS!
Grandma has started composing songs about sewing machines.

She is now known as a Singer Songwriter, or sew it seems.

HEY, KIDS!
The calculator that I have had for years has just stopped working. I have no idea why.
It's always been reliable.

It just doesn't add up.

HEY, KIDS!
I once had a girlfriend who broke up with me when she discovered that I only had 9 toes.

Apparently, she was lack toes intolerant.

HEY, KIDS!
My dad died because no one could remember his blood type. As he was dying, he was still being as encouraging as he always had been. He kept telling us "Be positive ". "Be positive". We really miss him.

HEY, KIDS!
When I was a butcher my main art form was to make portrait shapes of famous people out of steaks.

It was a rare medium, but really well done.

HEY, KIDS!
Grandma said that she is sick of my jokes and animal puns.

I told her "Alpaca my bags".

HEY, KIDS!
I decided to throw in my job as a personal trainer because I am not strong enough. I had to give them my too weak notice.

HEY, KIDS!
I saw a woman standing in the middle of a tennis court. I knew immediately that she must be Annette.

HEY, KIDS!
Do you remember the joke I told you about the Chiropractor?

It was about a weak back.

HEY, KIDS!
Do you know what is made of leather and sounds like a sneeze? A-SHOE

HEY, KIDS!
Grandma and I went to the wedding of two antennas. The service was okay but the reception was excellent.

HEY, KIDS!
Iamonthemoonandthereisnoplacetogetabeer.

Thereisnospacebar.

HEY, KIDS!
Gravity is one of the most powerful forces in the universe. But what happens if you remove it?

You're left with gravy.

HEY, KIDS!
I asked Siri, "Why am I not very good at getting women?"

She replied, "I'm Alexa you Moron".

HEY, KIDS!
Why can't Harry Potter tell the difference between his cooking pot and his best friend?

Because they are both cauld-Ron.

HEY, KIDS!
A group of butts is walking along a street. The smallest one is struggling to keep up. Sorry, he says, I'm a little behind.

HEY, KIDS!
So what if I can't spell Armageddon. It's not the end of the world.

HEY, KIDS!
A man trained a wolf to sit and listen to instructions.

Now he's aware wolf.

HEY, KIDS!
Grandma asked me if I could clear the table.
I had to get a running start but I made it.

HEY, KIDS!
My Grandma was 80% Irish. So, we called her Iris.

HEY, KIDS!
Why is a room full of married people
considered to be empty?

Because in reality there is not a single person there.

HEY, KIDS!
I was wondering why there was music 🎵 coming out of
my printer. Then I realised that it's just
the paper jamming again.

HEY, KIDS!
If you need to kill a French Vampire you have to drive
a baguette through its heart. Sounds easy but the
process is pain staking.

HEY, KIDS!
I asked the cook at the restaurant how they
prepare their chicken.

He replied. We keep it simple, we just tell them
they are going to die.

HEY, KIDS!
It's Grandma's birthday soon and she has started to
leave jewellery catalogues all around the house.

I think that I have got it right this time. I have bought
her a MAGAZINE RACK.

HEY, KIDS!
We were in the supermarket looking at the turkeys for Christmas. They all looked rather small. Grandma asked, "Do they get any bigger"? I replied "No, they're dead".

HEY, KIDS!
I heard that by law you have to turn on your headlights when it's raining in Sweden.

How in the heck am I supposed to know when it's raining in Sweden.

HEY, KIDS!
I once got fired from my job at the Calendar Company.

All I did was take a few days off.

HEY, KIDS!
When I was working my boss said that he was highly suspicious of why I only got sick on week days.

I told him that it must be my weekend immune system.

HEY, KIDS!
What does a CIA Agent do when he needs some sleep?

He goes undercover.

HEY, KIDS!
Why should you never sing in the shower?

Because 🎵 singing leads to dancing. Dancing leads to slipping and slipping leads to Paramedics seeing you naked. How embarrassment.

HEY, KIDS!
I asked my doctor before my surgery. How often do people die from this procedure?

He said, only once.

HEY, KIDS!
A dad told his little daughter to go to bed. She asked why? The dad told her it was because the cows were sleeping in the paddock.
What has that got to do with me going to bed, she asked.

It's pasture bed time.

HEY, KIDS!
Don't ever throw sodium chloride at people.

That's a salt.

HEY, KIDS!
I'm reading a great book about antigravity.

It's impossible to put down.

HEY, KIDS!
An old lady walked into a bank. Ouch. She asked the bank manager if he could check her balance.

So, the bank manager pushed her.

Her balance wasn't bad.

HEY, KIDS!
Do you know the name of the lady who decided to set fire to all her bills?

Bernadette.

HEY, KIDS!
Did you know that the Swordfish has no known natural predators except for the Penfish, which is known to be mightier.

HEY, KIDS!
I ate a kid's meal at McDonalds this morning for breakfast.

His mum was not very happy.

HEY, KIDS!
When I was working, my boss was always at me about being more creative. Then he died. I can remember at his funeral, I was looking at him lying in his coffin and couldn't help saying. "Guess who's thinking outside the box now Harry ".

HEY, KIDS!
Grandma is mad at me because I never buy her flowers. I can never win. I didn't even know she was selling flowers.

HEY, KIDS!
The other day the doctor said to me, can we talk about your weight?

Yes, I said, I think that's a very good idea. It was over 60 minutes today but at least this time I had a chair.

HEY, KIDS!
Did you know that my father was born a conjoined twin but the doctors managed to separate them at birth.

So, I have an uncle once removed.

HEY, KIDS!
I stayed up all night thinking and wondering where the sun went. Then it dawned on me.

HEY, KIDS!
What part of the hospital should you never undress in?

ICU.

HEY, KIDS!
You know the banks should do a better job at keeping their ATMs filled. I went to 5 yesterday and they all said "insufficient funds".

HEY, KIDS!
My Barber just got arrested for selling drugs. I have been a customer for 3 years and I never knew he was a barber.

HEY, KIDS!
Your Grandma asked me to pass her lipstick and I accidentally passed her a glue stick. Now she is acting stuck up and won't talk to me.

HEY, KIDS!
What do you call a paper airplane that won't fly?

STATIONARY.

HEY, KIDS!
Grandma told me that she saw a deer on the way to the supermarket.

Grandma never ceases to amaze me. How did she know it was going to the supermarket?

HEY, KIDS!
Since Covid, my going out clothes have missed me a lot. I put them on yesterday and they hugged me so tightly I could hardly move.

HEY, KIDS!
Why do Hairdressers make good Taxi drivers?
They know all the short cuts.

HEY, KIDS!
A wood chopper went into a forest to chop down some trees. He is about to make his first chop when the tree yells out. "Stop, you can't kill me I'm a talking tree".

The wood chopper stops and thinks for a moment before he says. "Yes you are, but you will dialogue".

HEY, KIDS!
Grandma and I went into a bar. A man comes up to me and asks. Would you like a drink for your wife?
I said, yes, that seems like a fair exchange.

HEY, KIDS!
Grandma bought me some coconut shampoo.
I don't know why. I don't even have a coconut.

HEY, KIDS!
I just told Grandma that I heard on the news that a famous actress killed herself.

Grandma asked me who was it?

I told her that I didn't quite hear the name but I think it was Reece somebody.

Grandma said not Witherspoon?

I said no, with a knife.

HEY, KIDS!
Did you know that justice is a dish best served cold.
If it was served warm it would be just water.

HEY, KIDS!
A young child was debating with his teacher the story of Jonah and the whale. The teacher was saying that it is impossible for a whale to swallow a human. When I get to heaven, I'll ask Jonah said the child. What if Jonah went to Hell asked the teacher.
Then you can ask him, said the child.

HEY, KIDS!
Grandma and I went out to a nice restaurant and we arrived about 10 minutes before our reservation time. The Manager asked, "would you mind waiting for a short time"? I told him it was okay and that we could wait. He said "Good, take these drinks to table 9".

HEY, KIDS!
I recently forgot my wedding anniversary. Grandma was so angry she said "tomorrow morning I want to see a gift in my driveway that goes from 0-200 in under 6 seconds". I got busy. The next morning Grandma looked outside and saw a big box, gift wrapped parked in the middle of the driveway. Grandma ran out all excited, opened it and found a new set of bathroom scales. Can I come and live at your place?

HEY, KIDS!
Two policemen are talking on a 2 way radio.

Policeman 1. The suspect has been spotted naked and dancing along Bourke Street.

Policeman 2. Copy that.

Policeman 1. I'll try, but I'm not a very good dancer.

HEY, KIDS!
How do you get a farm girl to marry you?
A TRACTOR.

HEY, KIDS!
The social distancing rules have caused an increase in mental health concerns for the members of the Flat Earth Society.
There are fears that they may be pushed over the edge.

HEY, KIDS!
The GPS in my new car told me to turn around. With all the so-called safety features in this car I think this feature is rather dangerous. Because, when I turned around, I couldn't see where I was going.

HEY, KIDS!
I visited a friend in his new house. He said, "Relax, make yourself at home. Think of this as if it's your own place". So, I did. I threw him out.
I hate visitors.

HEY, KIDS!
Some people say I'm self-centred.
But that's enough about them.

HEY, KIDS!
Grandma asked me to put tomato sauce on the shopping list. I did and now she is complaining that she can't read it.

HEY, KIDS!
I once invited a friend home for dinner without telling Grandma. Grandma got angry and started to yell at me. "My hair and makeup are not done, I'm not dressed for visitors, the house is not clean, we don't have enough food in the house to feed him, why did you bring him home?" I told her,

"He is thinking of getting married and I wanted to give him a demo".

HEY, KIDS!
A dog owner is chastising his dog. "The Neighbour tells me that you have been chasing people on a bicycle". The dog looks back with sad eyes and says, "He's lying, I don't even have a bicycle".

HEY, KIDS!
Grandma and I went out to dinner. I said to Grandma, see that waitress over there, I think she likes me. Grandma said, be careful stay away from her, she has COVID. Why do you say that I asked?
Because she has no taste.

HEY, KIDS!
You should have seen the look on the cashier's face when I bought a box of bird seed and asked her how long do they take to grow after I have planted them?

HEY, KIDS!
When I was at the Carnival, I saw a rather pudgy psychic. I think he was a Four Chin Teller.

HEY, KIDS!
Did you hear about the kidnapping at school?
It's fine, he eventually woke up.

HEY, KIDS!
Two little kids were talking about marriage when one asked. How many wives can one man have. The other started counting on his fingers and then said 16 I think. Four better, four worse, four richer and four poorer.

HEY, KIDS!
After being diagnosed with Diabetes I went on the Diabetes Website. The first thing they asked me was "Do you accept cookies"? Is this a trick question?

HEY, KIDS!
Did you hear about the Optician who was asked to make a pair of glasses for Andre the Giant.

Apparently, he made a huge spectacle.

HEY, KIDS!
What is Mr Nosmo King most famous for?

Having his name printed on more
signs than anybody else.

HEY, KIDS!
You're Australian when you enter the toilet. You're Australian when you come out of the toilet. Do you know what you are while you're in there? European.

HEY, KIDS!
Why did the drowning Pharaoh refuse help?
He was in denial.

HEY, KIDS!
I asked Grandma, is this safe to eat?
No, it's not she said, it's to put our valuables in.

HEY, KIDS!
I was having my regular check-up at the doctors.
"Do you think I will have a long and healthy life?" I asked. "I doubt it", the doctor said, shaking his head.
"Mercury is in Uranus right now ".
"I don't believe in all that astrology stuff Doc",
I told him.
"Neither do I" said the doctor,
"but my thermometer just broke".

HEY, KIDS!
Did you know that if gardeners didn't plant bulbs the worms wouldn't be able to see where they are going?

HEY, KIDS!
Did you know that according to Japanese folk lore the colour of a person's aura changes just before they die.

Cyan-aura.

HEY, KIDS!
Some people always need their opinions validated.
Am I right?

HEY, KIDS!
My pet goat used to eat cans of adhesive.
But now it's glue tin free.

HEY, KIDS!
I went out for a coffee. It was the worse coffee ever, it tasted like mud. So, I did a Grandma and complained.
I told them, "this coffee tastes like mud".
He said, "well it should,
it was only fresh ground this morning".

HEY, KIDS!
I just realized that one of you has grown up quickly and will be 18 this year. I thought we might all like to put in and buy her one of those locket things that you can put a picture in. We can put a picture of her in it and she can wear it around her neck.

Then she will really be in-de-pendant.

HEY, KIDS!
Ever since I ran over a chicken with my lawn mower, I have been seeing some weird and scary things.
I think that I may have a poultrygeist.

HEY, KIDS!
Did you know that if you want to become a garbage man you don't have to do any official training.
You just pick up things on the job as you go.

HEY, KIDS!
Grandma told me to get the invitation from the bench and go and buy what we needed for the party.
So, I went to the butcher and brought an Ox tongue.
The invitation clearly said Casual attire,
bring your own liquor. Grandma not impressed again.

HEY, KIDS!
Did you know that I have this bad habit of drinking brake fluid. Don't worry because I
can stop any time I want.

HEY, KIDS!
Within minutes of arriving at the crime scene the super detective was able to identify the murder weapon.
It was a brief case.

HEY, KIDS!
A Dung Beetle walks into a bar. Is this stool taken?

HEY, KIDS!
Yesterday I found a cockroach in the kitchen. I spent hours cleaning and scrubbing everything down thoroughly. Today Grandma put it in the bathroom.

HEY, KIDS!
A professional poker player lost his arm in an accident.
They fitted him with a prosthetic arm.
He was finding it very difficult to deal with.

HEY, KIDS!
I just noticed my new calendar has only 11 months.
I am dismayed.

HEY, KIDS!
Do you know that I still have it and I keep dazzling the women. I go to the shopping Centres and the cashiers are always checking me out.

HEY, KIDS!
I just discovered the leading cause of dry skin.
It's Towels.

HEY, KIDS!
I decided to do some research and write a book about winds, hurricanes and storms.
It's only a draft at the moment.

HEY, KIDS!
I was so hungry last night Grandma said that I ate my dinner like a computer. Megabytes.

HEY, KIDS!
At a local restaurant the waiter asked me, how would you like your steak cooked Sir?
I replied, like winning an argument with Grandma.

"Then rare it is Sir".

HEY, KIDS!
What do you call a Priest who studies to become a Lawyer? Father-in-law.

HEY, KIDS!
Years ago when I was a train driver, they held an enquiry in to the many accidents I was having. How can you explain all these derailments,
they asked.
I told them I don't know, it's hard to keep track.

HEY, KIDS!
We got stopped by the police the other day while your Grandma was driving. The policeman looked at Grandma's license and said, "this license states that you should be wearing glasses". "I have contacts" your Grandma stated using her angry voice. "Don't you threaten me Madam", the Policeman responded.

HEY, KIDS!
Here are some things to do on your holidays. Swimming with the dolphins? Swimming with the sharks? Did you know that swimming with the sharks is more expensive than swimming with the dolphins? One guy told me that it cost him an arm and a leg.

HEY, KIDS!
I found a book with the title "How to solve 50% of your problems". I bought 2.

HEY, KIDS!
A Pirate goes to the doctor to check some growths
on his skin. Nothing to worry about says the doctor,
they're benign. Look again says the Pirate,
I think you'll find there be ten. RRR.

HEY, KIDS!
I hate being dyslexic. You mix up two letters
and your whole sentence is urined.

HEY, KIDS!
Grandma and I went grocery shopping together.
I picked up a carton of 24 beers on special for $10.
Grandma tells me to put them back because
we can't afford it.

A few aisles later Grandma picks up a jar
of beauty cream for $20.

I told her to put it back we can't afford it.

Using her sweet voice Grandma says "but it makes me
look beautiful".
I said, "so does 24 cans of beer and they're
only half the price".

HEY, KIDS!
I have discovered that my lawn is chicken proof.
It's impeccable.

HEY, KIDS!
In the old days when I was at school and still had
much to learn about many things not using correct
punctuation such as commas and full stops when
writing was considered a serious crime and it often
resulted in a long sentence.

HEY, KIDS!
A blind guy is sitting having a drink at a bar. He calls out to the bloke sitting next to him "do you want to hear a blonde joke?"

The bloke next to him says, "before you tell that joke there's something you should know. The bartender is blonde, the bouncer is blonde, I'm blonde, the bloke sitting on your other side is 6 foot tall, plays rugby and he is blonde, his mate next to him is a professional wrestler and he's blonde.

Are you sure you want to tell that joke?"
Na, says the blind guy, "I don't want to have to explain it 5 times."

HEY, KIDS!
I never thought my chiropractor could improve my posture. But I stand corrected.

HEY, KIDS!
Did you know that Grandma likes to think she is modern and up with the times. The other day I asked her to pass me a phone book. She laughed at me, called me a dinosaur and passed me her iPhone instead. Well now the spider is dead,
her iPhone is broken and she is not very happy.

HEY, KIDS!
A Policeman came to the door last night and said he was looking for a man with one eye. I told him that he would probably find him quicker if he used both.

HEY, KIDS!
I just finished building a model of the Sydney Harbor Bridge. Grandma asked me if it is to scale.
I told her no, it's just to look at.

HEY, KIDS!
When I was at school, we were doing a lesson on words starting with the letter D. The teacher asked me to write a sentence that used the words defence, defeat and detail in it. I wrote
"When a horse jumps over defence, defeat go over first and detail comes last".

HEY, KIDS!
I declare the 24th of July a worldwide holiday.
No one should have to work 24/7.

HEY, KIDS!
Did you know that people are lazy when it comes to spelling. Like when people write congrats instead of congradulashons.

HEY, KIDS!
I went skydiving today for the first time. I was a little nervous. On the way up this guy came up to me and strapped us together. Then we jumped.
As we plummeted the guy asked me
"So how long have you been an instructor?"

HEY, KIDS!
When my mother-in-law came to dinner she asked me why the dog was staring at her? I told her it was because she was using his plate.

HEY, KIDS!
I'm really tired of people complaining about the price of everything. $4 for a cup of coffee, add 50 cents for sugar. Biscuits an extra dollar. Parking $5.
I think I'll just have to stop inviting them over if they are going to complain.

HEY, KIDS!
Not sure if your Grandma knows much about Geography but Alaska.

HEY, KIDS!
I was referred to a therapist who asked me, what brings you in today?

I told him that I have developed a real fear of tsunamis.

The Therapist asked me, how severe is it?

I told him that I'm not sure, it comes in waves.

HEY, KIDS!
I just realized why the ducks always bite my dog when I take him to the lake. It's because he's pure bread.

HEY, KIDS!
When Grandma went to a therapist, she was told to embrace her mistakes. She came straight home and gave me a big hug. How nice.

HEY, KIDS!
An old lady is sitting near the driver on a bus. Every few minutes she offers the driver some peanuts. The driver thanks her as he happily munches away and asks her why she doesn't eat them herself. "I can't" said the old woman, "I have no teeth".
"Then why do you buy them" the driver asks.
"Oh, I just love that chocolate they put around them."

HEY, KIDS!
Grandma has gone on a tropical diet.
The pantry is full of weird tropical stuff.
It's enough to make a mango crazy.

HEY, KIDS!
It's been pouring raining for 3 days and Grandma is getting depressed. She just stands there and stares through the window.
If things don't improve soon,
I'll have to let her in.

HEY, KIDS!
Did I ever tell you that when I first met your Grandma, she was a radiologist. I met her when I had to go in for an x-ray. I wonder what she saw in me.

HEY, KIDS!
Do you know who is taller Mr Bigger or his son?
His son is. He was known to be a little bigger ever since he was born.

HEY, KIDS!
When I was growing up, I had a friend named Tony. He was nice but a bit weird. Whenever we would see each other the first thing he would always say was. "Please don't say my name backwards again.
And I would always reply Y not?

HEY, KIDS!
The reopening of Lego World this year was a really really big thing. It created so much interest that people were lined up for blocks.

HEY, KIDS!
When I was a kid, I wanted to play the guitar really badly. After years of hard work and practice I can now play the guitar really badly. It goes to show you that hard work really pays off.

HEY, KIDS!
When I was younger, I got a job as a Waiter.
It wasn't a really flash job but what the heck,
it put food on the table.

HEY, KIDS!
Grandma laughs at my jokes when I tell them to her face. But she will not laugh if I send them in a text.
I decided to ask her why. She told me
"your jokes are not remotely funny".

HEY, KIDS!
I have just found out I am a social vegan.
This is based on the fact that I avoid meets. Interesting.

HEY, KIDS!
The Mother's Day awards for next year will include a new category for the shortest mum in the world.
We will call it the minimum.

HEY, KIDS!
I have just discovered a Bogan's seafood diet for the weekend. They have Flake on Saturday,
Whiting on Sundy and Barramundi.

HEY, KIDS!
I grilled a chicken for over 2 hours.
It still wouldn't tell me why it crossed the road.

HEY, KIDS!
You know that smoking will kill you don't you.

Did you know that bacon will also kill you.

However, smoking bacon will cure it.

HEY, KIDS!
I always knew that maths was stupid. I just realized that 10 + 10 and 11 + 11 equal the same.
10 + 10 = 20 and 11 + 11 = 20 too.

HEY, KIDS!
Last night I had a bad dream about drowning in an orange ocean. I was okay,
I realized it was only in a Fanta Sea.

HEY, KIDS!
Grandma and I had this big argument. Grandma got so angry she shouted at me to get out. She told me that she hopes that I die a long, slow and painful death.
I was confused. What, now she wants me to stay.

HEY, KIDS!
I asked Grandma to help me with a crossword puzzle. The clue was "overworked postman".

How many letters she asked. Der, obviously too many.

HEY, KIDS!
I really enjoy and am fascinated by the way the earth rotates. It really makes my day.

HEY, KIDS!
Many years ago Grandma became concerned that our first child looked nothing at all like her or me. Grandma was so concerned that she arranged a DNA test which revealed that the child was not ours. In discussing this I needed to remind her what had happened back when we were leaving the hospital. "Don't you remember, when we were leaving the hospital, the baby pooped and you told me to go back in and change him. I only did what you said. I went back inside took a clean one and left the dirty one there".

HEY, KIDS!
Some advice for all my grandchildren. Do not marry a tennis player, love means nothing to them.

HEY, KIDS!
You technically minded young people may be able to help me. I am trying to turn off the auto correct function on your Grandma.

HEY, KIDS!
I once had a job in a toy factory. My role was casting plastic Dracula's. There was only two of us on this assembly line so I had to make every second count.

HEY, KIDS!
I now have a pet pony. I call him Mayo.
Sometimes Mayo Neighs.

HEY, KIDS!
I met a man on a plane. He looked over at me and said, "you look nervous, is this your first time?"
I replied, "No, I have been nervous many times before."

HEY, KIDS!
Did you know that my grandfather was always terrible to me until I became a dad. All of a sudden, he became a great grandfather.

HEY, KIDS!
I once applied for a job as the head man at Old McDonalds Farm. If I got the job, I would have been the CIEIO.

HEY, KIDS!
Does anyone want a lot of used batteries?
Free of charge.

HEY, KIDS!
I worked for a short while in a fruit shop.
The conditions were poor but the celery was good.

HEY, KIDS!
Yesterday your grandma sent me a text out of the blue.
It simply said "your great". I texted her back saying "no,
no, no, you're great". She wandered around all day
with a big smile having a really good day.
I now don't have the heart to tell her that I was
only correcting her grammar.

HEY, KIDS!
I just found out that Bruce Lee had a younger brother
who is believed to move even faster than Bruce.
His name is Sudden Lee.

HEY, KIDS!
Bruce Lee had a second brother Broco Lee.
No one liked him much.

HEY, KIDS!
Bruce also had a sister who was always very bouncy
and happy. Mary Lee.

HEY, KIDS!
Bruce Lee said his youngest brother is a really
great guy. Friend Lee.

HEY, KIDS!
Bruce Lee's cousin is not so fortunate. Ug Lee.
Not a pretty sight.

HEY, KIDS!
Bruce Lee's other cousin is a bit over weight.
Broad Lee.

HEY, KIDS!
Not all Bruce Lee's brothers were as hard or tough as Bruce. One of them was named Soft Lee.

HEY, KIDS!
When Bruce Lee first started his training, he would sit and watch his Grandfather train for hours at a time. His Grandfather would go over and over the same move until he got it right. His name was Repeated Lee.

HEY, KIDS!
Bruce Lee's wife was very caring and loving.

Compassionate Lee.

HEY, KIDS!
Another of Bruce's cousins was not very good and making slow, if any improvement.
They called him Marginal Lee.

HEY, KIDS!
Do you realize that nothing is made in Australia any more. I just got a new TV and it says "built in Antenna". I don't even know where that is.

HEY, KIDS!
I was at an op shop and saw a man stuffing a big toy lion and a witch doll into a big old wardrobe.
I was curious so I asked him what he was doing. He told me to go away, "it's nania business." How rude!

HEY, KIDS!
Do you know why you should never brush your teeth
with your left hand? It's because a tooth brush
does a much better job.

HEY, KIDS!
Did you know that the adjective for metal is metallic.
Therefore, the adjective for iron must be ironic.

HEY, KIDS!
A little preppy was doing a drawing of his dad.
The teacher asked, "how old is your dad?"
The kid thought for a minute then said he's 5.
"No," said the teacher "he can't be a dad when he is 5".
The kid replied "that's because he only became
a dad when I was born." Smart kid.

HEY, KIDS!
My dog is very smart. I asked him a question the other
day. If I give you two bones and then take two away,
how many will you have left?
It might surprise you but he said nothing.

HEY, KIDS!
Birthdays are good for your health.
Statistics say that people who have them live longer.

HEY, KIDS!
Did you know that I went to Sailor's school.
Unfortunately, I failed.
They tried to teach me the alphabet
but I kept getting lost at C.

HEY, KIDS!
Grandma told me if I bought her one more meaningless gift, she would burn it.

So, I bought her a candle.

HEY, KIDS!
I accidentally drank a bottle of invisible ink last night and now I am at the hospital waiting to be seen.

HEY, KIDS!
A German visitor once jumped into a river to save a drowning dog. He said to the dog owner "here is ze dog, dry him off keep him warm and he vil be fine". The owner thanked him and asked "are you a vet?" "Vet, of course I'm vet, I've been in river you vidiot."

HEY, KIDS!
I was just admiring my roof. I'm not sure if it is the best roof in the world but it's definitely up there.

HEY, KIDS!
My new doctor was asking about my medical history. Have you ever had any serious injuries or accidents? I told her that I once broke my arm in three places. The doctor said the best advice I can give you to avoid that happening again is not to go to those places.

HEY, KIDS!
Why is the word dark spelt with a K?
Isn't it obvious. it's because you can't c in the dark.

HEY, KIDS!
Grandma and I went out to dinner last night. The waitress came over and asked, do you want to hear today's special? I said yes please.
She replied, "alright, Today is special".

HEY, KIDS!
I was wondering, if a cow doesn't produce milk is it a sick cow or an udder failure?

HEY, KIDS!
For our anniversary I took Grandma out to a fruit orchard. We just stood there staring at the fruit on the trees for nearly an hour. I found out later that this wasn't the Apple Watch she was wanting.

HEY, KIDS!
I was trying to think of something witty to say to my neighbour who just got a new job as a cabinet maker. I needed something that woodwork. I think I nailed it but unfortunately no one saw it.

HEY, KIDS!
My therapist told me to write letters to everyone who has ever hurt me and then burn them. I have done this but now I don't know what to do with the letters.

HEY, KIDS!
I found an old Science test from my school days.

Question 3. Why do bees stay in their hives in winter?

My answer. Swarm.

I was a very clever kid.

HEY, KIDS!
Grandma texted me the other frosty morning.
Windows frozen and won't open.

I texted her back. Just pour some warm water over the screen and it should be alright.
She texted back 10 minutes later.
Great advice the computer is really stuffed now.

HEY, KIDS!
Grandma just opened the car door for me.
My initial thought was how nice. But on further thought it would have been nicer if we weren't going 80km an hour at the time.

HEY, KIDS!
I discovered how to make a water bed bouncier.
All you do is use spring water.

HEY, KIDS!
Did you know that there are rules about starting a Zoo?
It's true. You are required to have at least two pandas, three Grizzlies and four Polars and that's the bear minimum.

HEY, KIDS!
I just learned that Shakespeare wrote all his plays using a pencil. What I didn't learn was, was it 2B or not 2B?

HEY, KIDS!
I went into the local police station and asked if I tickle a man to death is it manslaughter?

HEY, KIDS!
Tonight I will be having Himalayan Rabbit Stew
for dinner. I found Himalayan on the road.

HEY, KIDS!
When I was looking around for my new car it was
important to have enough room for our suitcases.
I asked this salesman, Cargo space?
He replied.
Car no can do that, car go road.

HEY, KIDS!
Grandma has started referring to me as her computer.
It's not because I'm smart, it's because I go to sleep
every 15 minutes if I'm unattended to.

HEY, KIDS!
Does anyone know why my post was removed?
It's really annoying because now my
fence is falling over.

HEY, KIDS!
I learn something new every day. I just learned that
bread is like the Sun.
It rises in the yeast and sets in the waist.

HEY, KIDS!
About 6 months ago I spent $50 for a book I bought
on line "How To Scam People". It hasn't arrived yet.

HEY, KIDS!
I always knew that ghosts don't eat so I was very
surprised to learn that they are heavy drinkers.
It's true they are really into their boos.

HEY, KIDS!
I have started a new project. I'm letting as many people as I can know about the health benefits of eating dried grapes. It's all about raisin awareness.

HEY, KIDS!
I just discovered why the clock in my kitchen is always wrong. It keeps going back for seconds.

HEY, KIDS!
Yesterday I got a text with IDK in it. I asked Grandma what it means. She said "I don't know", so now I am asking everybody else.

HEY, KIDS!
Grandma accused me of cheating when she found all the letters I was hiding. Then she got very angry and told me that she would never play scrabble with me again.

HEY, KIDS!
When I was a kid we had 2 Doberman dogs. One was named Rolex the other was Timex. They were watch dogs 🐶.

HEY, KIDS!
Last week Grandma started reading The Exorcist. She told me that it was the most evil book she has ever tried to read. She didn't finish it. She was so disgusted with it she took it on one of our walks and threw it in the lake at the end of our street.

I had another copy she didn't know about so I found it, soaked it in a bucket of water for an hour and then placed it on her bedside table right next to her bed. I don't think she will sleep well tonight.

HEY, KIDS!
Yesterday your Grandma asked me why I was sitting down while doing the dishes. I told her it was because I can't stand doing them.

HEY, KIDS!
There's another new development in how to open a car. Great new technology. All you do is choose the correct paint colour and it will open by itself.
As long as it is Khaki.

HEY, KIDS!
I just found out that they wore wigs way back in the biblical days. I read it last night. The story said that Moses went to speak with Pharaoh with Aaron.

HEY, KIDS!
I remember one day long ago when your Grandma was younger, she came in and told me that her ear was hurting. I asked her if it was hurting inside or out. She turned around and walked out the back door. Grandma was only out there for a few seconds before she came back in. She then said, "both".

HEY, KIDS!
The first humans would watch the sun rise in the east and set in the west. They did this over and over again, watching the cycle. Eventually they got bored and called it a day

HEY, KIDS!
I used to be in a band called Books. Unfortunately, everybody would judge us by our covers.

HEY, KIDS!

Last time your Grandma and I had a check-up at the doctors we raised the concern about our memories. The doctor said that at our age the best thing to do is get in the habit of writing things down. Well last night we got the chance to test it. I got up to go to the kitchen and Grandma asked me to get her a bowl of strawberries and to write it down. I told her that I didn't need to. She insisted that I write it down because she also wanted some ice cream and a cup of tea. I told her I could manage it. Well ten minutes later I brought in her order of bacon and eggs and she was not happy. "I told you to write it down she said. I knew you would forget, where's my toast?"

HEY, KIDS!

Now that I'm retired with extra time on my hands I sometimes think about stupid things for hours. The other day I found myself thinking about how much a rainbow would weigh. All I could come up with is that I know it's pretty light.

HEY, KIDS!

In Australia we have lifts but when I was in America they referred to them as elevators. The only reason that I can think of it must be in the different ways we are raised.

HEY, KIDS!

If you want to have fun with the family make some funny bone soup. It becomes laughing stock.

HEY, KIDS!

I'm throwing a ball for our dog. It's a bit extravagant but it's his birthday soon and he looks great in a tux.

HEY, KIDS!
This is a message to the person who pushed into the queue line in front of me. I'm after you now.

HEY, KIDS!
Grandma told me that the Prime Minister of Canada has been re-elected. I thought she was lying at first, but it's Trudeau.

HEY, KIDS!
Do you realise that the English language is really stupid. When we send something by road we call it a shipment, but when we send something by ship, we call it cargo.

HEY, KIDS!
Why do you not need to include BYO on a party invitation being held in a haunted house?
It's because the ghosts supply the boos.

HEY, KIDS!
3 conspiracy theorists walk into a bar. Ouch.
You can't tell me that's a coincidence!

HEY, KIDS!
Do you know why the art thief's vehicle ran out of fuel?

It because he had no Monet to buy DeGas to make the Van Gough.

HEY, KIDS!
When my son was born, I wanted to name him Driew. Grandma said, don't you mean Drew? I said no Driew. She said you can't call him that it's weird. But I pointed out to her that it's only weird if you say it backwards.

HEY, KIDS!
When you die people say all these wonderful things about you. They say things like "I would give anything if only you would come back".

The funny thing is that when you do come back, they scream and run away.

HEY, KIDS!
Grandma and I found a lamp with a genie in it and we were granted one wish each. Grandma wished for a luxurious cruise. All of a sudden 2 cruise tickets appear in her hand. I looked at Grandma and wished she was 30 years younger than me.

All of a sudden, I was 92.

HEY, KIDS!
I once had a job at a keyboard factory on the assembly line. I wasn't there long. I got fired.
They said I wasn't putting in enough shifts.

HEY, KIDS!
Yesterday I sent a text message to your Grandma asking her a simple question. She is trying to get all trendy and modern now. She texted back IDK ILY TTYL. So, I text her back. "?".

Then she says I don't know. I love you. Talk to you later. So, I said that's all right I ask the grandchildren.

HEY, KIDS!
Why do you need to be extra, extra, extra careful if you have to reverse a Subaru?
Because literally you are a bus backwards.
U R A BUS

HEY, KIDS!
You know how sports people throw a ball into the
crowd in celebration when they win the game.
I tried that but apparently you are not allowed
to do it in 10 pin bowling.
Biggest strike I ever had.
Now they won't let me play.

HEY, KIDS!
Yesterday Grandma was spotted by the police knitting
while she was driving. The police drove up beside her
and yelled "pullover". Grandma just smiled,
wound down the window and said
"No! It's a scarf."

HEY, KIDS!
Have you ever woken up feeling really good about life
and then kissed the person beside you?
Not a good idea. I did this one time and I have
never been allowed to fly that airline again.

HEY, KIDS!
A very stern looking policeman came to my door last
night and demanded that I tell him where
I was between 4 and 5.
He was not a happy man when I answered

"Kindergarten".

HEY, KIDS!
I am starting to feel very, very, old.
The other day I was driving past the cemetery
and my GPS told me
"You have reached your final destination".

HEY, KIDS!
I went to the doctor because I was convinced there was something wrong with my brain. I told the doctor that every time I take a drink of coffee, I get this stabbing pain in my eye. The doctor told me it was a common condition and the remedy was easy.
Just remove the spoon from the cup before you drink.

HEY, KIDS!
Do you know why the Army is so secretive?
I have been trying to do some research into the different ranks and want to start at the lowest rank and work up. I have asked about a dozen people now what is the lowest rank in the Army, and without exception they all said, it is private.
Maybe if I ring the recruitment line,
they will tell me.

HEY, KIDS!
Two monocles come together. One says to the other. "You know if we get together, we can make a spectacle of ourselves".

HEY, KIDS!
Did you know that it's really okay to talk to yourself.
And it's really okay to answer yourself as well.
But it's really sad when you need to repeat what you said because you weren't listening.

HEY, KIDS!
I am finding it's getting much harder to think quickly.
My neighbour said "think quick, what is the ninth letter of the alphabet"?
I became confused and just took a guess.
But you won't believe it but I was right.

HEY, KIDS!
I saw a couple of guys out in the street having a fight, if
you can believe it, over a bus ticket.
I didn't intervene because it was a fare fight.

HEY, KIDS!
For Christmas this year I decided to buy you all $150
worth of scratchies for the $50,000,000 lottery.
I was so excited that I scratched them all
myself to see what you won.
You will be excited to know that the $2 you won
is in the card I'll put under the Christmas tree.
Love Grandad.

HEY, KIDS!
I just bought a new book. "101 ways to get
glue off your hands".
It's not the best book I've ever read but I
can't put it down.

HEY, KIDS!
I discovered how Bilbo survived through the entire
Lord of the Rings trilogy.
It's because old hobbits die hard.

HEY, KIDS!
I might not be able to send you jokes for a few days.
The police are investigating me for
stealing pool accessories.
I'm going to have to lilo.

HEY, KIDS!
For Christmas this year I would like a seniors GPS. I
need one that will not only tell me how to get there
but why I went there. On second thought don't worry,
I have got Grandma.

HEY, KIDS!
Grandma and I were riding our bikes through the countryside and we could hear all this laughter coming from across the paddocks. We rode nearer to find the source and then I had to explain to Grandma that it was only Laughing Stock.

HEY, KIDS!
Do you know that Elon Musk, the founder of Tesla, is from South Africa. I thought he was from Mad-a-gas-car.

HEY, KIDS!
Grandma and I were down the beach and we just saw a car being driven by a sheep wearing a swimsuit. It was a Lambakini.

HEY, KIDS!
I found Grandma calmly talking to our front door as if she was negotiating terms. I asked her what she was doing and she explained that she had locked herself out. She told me that she had learnt through her Counsellor that if she had a problem, calm communication is the key.

HEY, KIDS!
At my last medical check-up my doctor asked me if there is a reason why I always wear 2 undies. I told him that I thought everyone did. My mother taught me never to go out without wearing a clean pair of socks and a pair of clean undies in case I get hit by a bus.

HEY, KIDS!
Now I am getting older I walk slowly with a walking stick. On those occasions when I am in a bit of a rush, I use a hurry cane.

HEY, KIDS!
I just found out that Santa has another reindeer. Olive. She doesn't get used much because apparently, she is not very nice to Rudolph. I don't understand why I didn't realise this before because it's in the song we all have been singing for years.

Olive the other reindeer used to laugh
and call him names.

HEY, KIDS!
Last Christmas we were in the city and we walked through the lobby of a big hotel. We overheard a group of chess fanatics all boasting about how good they were at the game. I remember saying to Grandma "there's nothing worse than chess nuts boasting in an open foyer".

HEY, KIDS!
Many years ago Grandma took you all to KFC. You all wanted a kid's meal with a leg. So, Grandma ordered 8 kid's meals with a leg. The lady behind the counter asked grandma, which side? Grandma hesitated and looked very confused. She said, it really doesn't matter, any side will do. The lady behind the counter told her that she had to choose. So, Grandma said she would have all right legs. The lady laughed and laughed. When she calmed down,
she said maybe I should ask chips or mash next time.

HEY, KIDS!
If you are thinking about Santa at the South Pole,
give up, it's a lost clause.

HEY, KIDS!
Yesterday in my spare time I invented the first thought controlled air freshener. It makes scents when you think about it.

HEY, KIDS!

Grandma was once participating in a radio quiz. The radio announcer said if she got the next question right, she would win $500. "Okay your question is…. Who was the first woman on earth?"

Grandma thought for a while and then asked for a hint. The radio announcer said, "all I can tell you is, think apples". "Okay, that's easy" Grandma said, "it's Granny Smith."

HEY, KIDS!

I just found out that the Norwegian Navy has barcodes on all their ships. Apparently, it so they can Scandinavian.

HEY, KIDS!

Something went wrong with our computer, AGAIN. I asked Grandma to help me sort it out. She fixed it in about 10 seconds. I asked what it was and she said it's the usual thing. What's the usual thing? I asked.
It's the ID ten T virus she told me.
Write it down so you don't forget.
So, I wrote it here so I won't forget it. ID10T.

HEY, KIDS!

I was seriously injured once while on holidays in France. I leaned too far over the balcony on a big tower. Unfortunately, Eiffel.

HEY, KIDS!

This year I got the best most fantastic Christmas present ever. It was a drum with no skin.

You just can't beat it.

HEY, KIDS!
I thought that I might get some crocodile meat for a special new year dinner, but then I remembered that I don't have a crockpot.

HEY, KIDS!
I just found out that the person who invented auto correct has died. The funeral is tomato.

HEY, KIDS!
An English man and an Irish man were working together. The English man comes up with a plan of how they can get the day off. Follow my lead says the English man who climbs into the rafters and hangs upside down. The boss comes in and asked what he was doing. I'm a light bulb the English man says. The boss looks concerned and tells him he better take the rest of the day off. As he climbs down and walks out the door the Irish man follows.
Where are you going the boss yells.
The Irish man calls back. I can't work in the dark.

HEY, KIDS!
I just learned a new magic trick. I now can make one disappear.
It's easy really you just add a G and it's Gone.

HEY, KIDS!
Grandma and I just found out that we don't need any more vaccinations. All we need to do is to get an anteater for a pet. Apparently, they are full of little antibodies.

HEY, KIDS!
Grandma and I decided to try one of those outside restaurants. It was a disaster. It started to rain and it really rained hard. If that wasn't bad enough it took me over 2 hours just to finish my soup.

HEY, KIDS!
I had a blind friend once. He asked to borrow $500 and promised to pay me back next time he saw me.

HEY, KIDS!
Did you know if you put socks on a bear,
it still has bear feet.

HEY, KIDS!
The only time I ever had a drink I got pulled over by a police woman. She told me to get out of the car. You're staggering, she said. I looked at her and said, well, you're quite beautiful yourself.
Please send bail money.

HEY, KIDS!
I once had a dog and I called him Minton. He loved to play. One day he ate my shuttlecock.
Bad- Minton.

HEY, KIDS!
I remember when one of you messaged me and told me that you had made some synonym buns.
I replied, "just like the one's grammar
used to make hey".
This Grandchild never talked to me for a week.

HEY, KIDS!
A pirate visits his favourite bar for the first time in a while. Haven't seen you for a while says the bartender. Are you alright? Yeah, really good says the pirate. What about the wooden leg says the bartender. Oh, that got blown off in a battle but it's all good now. And I noticed the hook on your arm, you didn't have that before says the bartender. Lost the hand in a sword fight says the pirate but really all is good now. And the eye patch asked the bartender, another battle scar? Oh no, says the pirate, a bird.
I was raising one of the sails on my jolly ship when a bird pooped in my eye. You lost an eye because a bird pooped in your eye? Asked the bartender.
No, no says the pirate,
it was the first day after I had the hook fitted.

HEY, KIDS!
A Vicks Vapor Rub truck has just rolled over on the Western Ring Road.
They are saying there will be no congestion
for up to 8 hours.

HEY, KIDS!
I was wondering, if the USA is so amazing why did someone need to invent a USB?

HEY, KIDS!
Who knows what Trav is short for?

Wrong. It's because he has little legs.

HEY, KIDS!
I have a new magic trick that I have just learned.
I can cut a piece of wood in half by just staring at it.
It's hard to believe but I actually saw
it with my own eyes.

HEY, KIDS!

I just found out that they had cars 🚗 back in the Bible times. If fact, Jesus drove a Honda.

He was rather secretive and didn't like to talk about it much. I discovered this in the Bible in the gospel of John 12 verse 49.
"For I did not speak of my own Accord."

HEY, KIDS!

I found a very large book in an op shop. The cover was nearly a meter and a half long and it was difficult for me to carry. I was very tired and really struggling, trying my best to manage and to get this book back to my car, worrying all the time how I am going to get this book into the car when I got there. The car was parked in a multi-storey car park on the 5th level right next to a big round concrete pillar about a kilometre from where I bought the book.

I knew that I wouldn't be able to open the passenger side door wide enough to get the book in the car from that side and was hoping that nobody was parked next to me on the other side. The book was so large that I was refused entry onto a tram. I accidentally bumped my book into a person who was extremely nice and kindly and generously offered to help me carry it. We walked and talked while he helped me carry my enormous large new book towards the car park where my car was parked on the 5th level next to a concrete pillar, He asked me "why do you want and what are you doing with such an enormous book?"

"It's a long story" I said.

HEY, KIDS!

Did I ever tell you about my pet pig I had as a kid? I called him Ink because he lived in a pen.

HEY, KIDS!
Grandma is singing in the house. I have decided to stay outside so the neighbours don't think I am hitting her.

HEY, KIDS!
One of my favourite childhood memories is building sand castles with my grandfather.
That was until my mother took the urn off me and told me that I couldn't play with him anymore.

HEY, KIDS!
I bought Grandma some flowers for Valentine's Day.
I thought she liked cauliflowers.
One day I will learn.

HEY, KIDS!
Grandma strikes back. She left me a note.

"Your dinner is in the recipe book page 102 and the ingredients are in the supermarket". Enjoy.

HEY, KIDS!
I am very compliant. I was about to pay for my groceries at the supermarket with my credit card.
The cashier said, "strip down facing me".
By the time I realized she was talking about the card it was too late.
Send more money for bail.

HEY, KIDS!
When I was younger, I decided not to become an archaeologist.
Someone told me that if I did my life would be in ruins.

HEY, KIDS!
Some Uber drivers can be touchy. The other day I called an Uber. He showed up and as we started off on our journey, he asked me, "do you mind if I put on some music?" "Not at all" I replied.
"Kiss" he said. "Let's listen to the music first and then see how we feel". "GET OUT!

HEY, KIDS!
Don't laugh at me because you think I'm crazy. Laugh at yourselves because you don't realise it's hereditary. Ha ha ha ha ha.

HEY, KIDS!
I just found out that I can lose weight just by wearing bread on my head.

Apparently, it is a loaf hat diet.

HEY, KIDS!
I decided to put a high voltage electric fence all the way around my house. My neighbour is dead against it.

HEY, KIDS!
I once got bitten by my dog. I googled "what to do, bleeding from a dog bite". Google told me "Elevate it and apply pressure". So, I picked up the dog, held it above my head and yelled. "Apologise or you won't get any dinner". It didn't work.

HEY, KIDS!
I was talking to Grandma about Koala bears. She told me that they are not really bears. Why aren't they? I asked. She told me

It's because they don't have the required koalafications.

HEY, KIDS!
I told Grandma that I wanted to be cremated.
She made an appointment for next Tuesday.

HEY, KIDS!
This morning I accidentally sprayed deodorant in my mouth thinking it was mouth wash.
Now I am talking with this weird axe-scent.

HEY, KIDS!
I remember many years ago coming home from work to find that my kids had been on eBay all day. I decided then and there that If they are still there the next day, I will lower the price.

HEY, KIDS!
Did I ever tell you that I married your Grandma because of her looks, but not for the ones she has been giving me lately.

HEY, KIDS!
Grandma once joined a secret cooking society. No one knew about it because it was a secret. Unfortunately, she didn't last long and got thrown out because she kept spilling the beans.

HEY, KIDS!
I was at the supermarket going through the checkout. The girl on the register asked me if I wanted the milk in a bag. She looked confused when I said
"no thanks, leave it in the carton".

HEY, KIDS!
I'm excited. I just purchased 75% of a vampire hunting business. That makes me the main stake holder.

HEY, KIDS!
Spider-Man has an evil twin brother who can never seem to pass his driver's test. Apparently, he is a bad parallel Parker.

HEY, KIDS!
I got robbed while at the petrol station yesterday. I called the police. They asked me if I knew who did it. I told them yes, it was pump 3.

HEY, KIDS!
I think I will write another book. This one will be about me and all the things I should have focused on and should have achieved in my life. It will be my personal oughtabiography.

HEY, KIDS!
Daffy Duck and Elmer Fud were robbing a liquor store when one picked up a bottle and asked the other. "Is this whisky?" The other said "yes, but not as whisky as wobbing a bank".

HEY, KIDS!
my neighbour just got a job in marketing for Kellogg's. His main role is Raisin Bran awareness.

HEY, KIDS!
Grandma believes that a guy wearing camouflage gear is very appealing. I just can't see it myself.

HEY, KIDS!
I am trying to remember a fish joke I shared a few years back. If you remember what it is please let minnow.

HEY, KIDS!
I asked my doctor why I always get heartburn when I eat birthday cake. Try eating it after you have taken the candles off, he said.

HEY, KIDS!
Not many people know about this but I used to be a boy trapped in a woman's body. It all worked out okay. After 9 months I was born.

HEY, KIDS!
It's only another 10 years until my pirate's birthday. That's when I can say Aye Matey

HEY, KIDS!
On my last birthday Grandma and I decided to have our first drink of wine. I had purchased a rather expensive bottle of red. After a few glasses Grandma said out loud "I love you".
I asked, "is that you or the wine talking?"
She said "it's me and I'm talking to the wine".

HEY, KIDS!
I went for a drive down to the beach for my birthday. I love the atmosphere and the greeting the ocean gives especially on special days. I was a little disappointed because the ocean had nothing to say to me this year, it only waved as I drove by.

HEY, KIDS!
I was not feeling well so I called into my GP. I told him that I was feeling a bit low. It's just old age he said. Don't worry, it doesn't last long.

HEY, KIDS!
I was not feeling well so I called into see my GP. He asked me a few questions and did a few tests. "Do you feel sweaty and light headed when you put petrol in your car? Do you feel anxious when you go to pay for it?" I said that I did. "I think you have Carowner Virus" he said. "You need to move into a freezer for a week and icealot."

HEY, KIDS!
The English language always provides something for us to ponder. Grandma and I were talking about vowels. Which vowel is the most important? Which vowel is the most used? Which vowel is the easiest to pronounce? The discussion was getting heated and was starting to turn into an argument, but in the end, I won. It's unusual but Grandma agreed. She said U won.

HEY, KIDS!
Every year Grandma keeps telling me to act my age. I need to keep reminding her that I don't know how, as I have never been this age before.

HEY, KIDS!
I am trying my luck at writing a romantic novel. It's about a farmer searching for love. Let me know what you think of my start. "Her body tensed and quivered as she felt wave after wave surge through it. I probably should have told her about the new electric fence".

HEY, KIDS!
Many, many, moons ago when my kids were small, I was at a shopping Centre with one of my daughters. I ran into an old friend and I introduced my daughter to him. "This is Kris" I said.
"Ok, what is Kris short for" he asked.
I replied "that might be because she's only three."

HEY, KIDS!
Many, many, moons ago when I was in the butchering business a woman came in and asked for an ox tail. I told her to take a seat and I began. Once upon a time there was this little ox named Oxscar……

HEY, KIDS!
Now that I am getting older, I have found that it's best if I drive a little faster. This way I can get there before I forget where I am going.

HEY, KIDS!
Many, many, moons ago I went for a job interview as a traveling salesman. The interviewer pointed to his laptop on his desk and said I want you to try and sell me this. I picked up the laptop and left.
He rang me a short time later asking for his laptop back. I said, that will be $1000. I got the job.

HEY, KIDS!
They tell us to remember our body is a temple. Look after it and treat it well they say. I just looked in the mirror. Mine is definitely a temple, it is ancient and crumbling, and looks like it is most possibly possessed and even haunted.
It's great being a relic.

HEY, KIDS!
I went to a restaurant and got my face slapped. All I did was call the waitress over and said "can I ask you something about the menu please?"
With that she just up and slapped me right across the face.
Ouch. She looked at me with anger in her eyes and said, "the men I please has nothing to do with you".

HEY, KIDS!
Grandma just cracked a funny. I asked her if I could eat that cake in the fridge. She said I could but I might be more comfortable in the lounge room.

HEY, KIDS!
Did you know that I haven't spoken to Grandma in over a year. It's not that I don't want to talk to her, it just that I don't like to interrupt her.

HEY, KIDS!
Many, many, moons ago when I was at school, I discovered one day that my English teacher was upset. She was a nice teacher and I didn't know what to say to make her feel better.
So, I decided to write her a note.

There, they're, their. It appeared to work.

HEY, KIDS!
Grandma recently told me that I look better without my glasses. I said, that's funny, you look better without my glasses too.

HEY, KIDS!
As I get older my ability to think quickly has diminished. I would like to thank all who were patient with me while I pondered and searched for the meaning of many. It means a lot.

HEY, KIDS!
As I get older my ability to think quickly and remember has diminished. I have been pondering the meaning of oblivious but I have to conclude, I have no idea.

HEY, KIDS!
There were 2 morons sitting on a fence. The bigger moron fell off. The other one didn't because he was a little moron.

HEY, KIDS!
When Grandma was at school, she told me that she failed an exam on Aboriginal 🎵 music.
I asked her Didja redo it? Ha ha.

HEY, KIDS!
I have decided to start a maths tutoring business for short people. I already have come up with a catchy slogan.

Make the little things count. Ha ha.

HEY, KIDS!
With the birth of all these beautiful babies the population of the world is growing so fast. I just read that the fastest growing city in the world right now is the capital of Ireland. In fact, it's Dublin.

HEY, KIDS!
When I decide to retire as the family joke teller, I am going to start an Apiary. It's sort of my plan bee.

HEY, KIDS!
Did you know that gravity is one of the most powerful forces known to us. However, when we remove it, we are left with just gravy.

HEY, KIDS!
I once had a dog I called Tenkay. People seemed impressed when I told them I walked Tenkay every day.

HEY, KIDS!
I have been working on my next travel plans. Thinking of places to go. I have never been to Cahoots but they say you shouldn't go alone. In fact, you have to be in Cahoots with someone. Also, I have never been in Cognito. Strange place, apparently no one recognises you there. However, I have been in Sane. You can't fly in, you have to be driven there.
It's a place I have been a lot over the years.

HEY, KIDS!
I just found out that Steph Graph's sister is named Poly. I'm not lying.

HEY, KIDS!
We went down to the local Chinese Restaurant for dinner. The place was packed. Never seen so many people there. Couldn't get a table. I said to the owner, what's going on here. She said it Tuyu's birthday.
I had to ask. Who's Tuyu? She said she didn't know but she heard them singing happy birthday Tuyu.

HEY, KIDS!
Another strange but interesting fact. Someone said that Sugar is the only English word that has a sh sound using the letters su. But when I think about that I am not so sure.

HEY, KIDS!
I have just gone through the contacts on my iPhone with the intention of cleaning them up. I can't believe how many contacts I had. Some I can't even remember. It looks like I had a lot of German friends at one time.
I don't remember any of them.
So, I decided to delete them all.
Now my phone is hansfree.

HEY, KIDS!
I had to go to the doctor because I had a blocked ear.
What ear is it? the doctor asked. I told him 2023.

HEY, KIDS!
We all know about the knights of the round table.
The big round one was known as Sir Comfrence.
However, I discovered another one hiding out the back
to avoid going into battle.
He was stuck up against the wall. Sir Render.

HEY, KIDS!
I've just discovered that I have another allergy.
Grandma cooked my breakfast and I realized that I am
Black Toast Intolerant.

HEY, KIDS!
On my walk yesterday I got attacked and bitten by
a bull terrier. When I got home Grandma was very
helpful and really concerned. She said, what if that had
been a small child? I don't know how weak she thinks I
am but I'm sure I could have fought off a small child.

HEY, KIDS!
Did you know I hated doing maths at school.
I once wrote a note to my maths teacher.

Dear Miss Algebra. Please stop asking me to find your
X. He's not coming back and I don't know Y.

HEY, KIDS!
When Grandma and I had a rental property, the tenant
rang me and told that he had a leak in the sink.
I told him that I really didn't need to know that,
and that I wouldn't judge him anyway.

HEY, KIDS!
I just showed Grandma my new magic trick.
I can now turn spaghetti into a 🚗 car. I couldn't make
it work at first but you should have seen the look on
Grandma's face when I drove pasta.

HEY, KIDS!
I'm thinking of starting a new career as a locksmith.
I just wrote a new song 🎵 that has a
lovely 🗝 key change.

HEY, KIDS!
I went and bought all new equipment to go camping
with Grandma. I decided to insure it all
to protect my investment.
However, I just found out that if someone steals my
tent in the middle of the night I'm not covered.

HEY, KIDS!
I was wondering what will happen to me if I get scared
half to death? Twice.

HEY, KIDS!
When I was a boy, my mother would send me to the
shops with $1. I would return home with a loaf of
bread, milk, biscuits, eggs, butter and jam.
I can't do it anymore, too many security cameras.

HEY, KIDS!
Another needless fact to ponder and add to your
useless information file. Incorrectly is a very interesting
word. It is the only word when spelt correctly
is still spelt incorrectly.

HEY, KIDS!
Two slices of bread were getting married.
The day was going really great until at their reception someone decided to toast the bride and groom.

HEY, KIDS!
I once had a friend who took a laxative with some holy water. I believe he started a religious movement.

HEY, KIDS!
Grandma came home all excited yesterday. She ran in the door yelling start packing your bags because I just won the lottery. I got all excited too and asked what should I pack, beach gear, walking shoes, dress clothes? She said it doesn't matter just get out.

HEY, KIDS!
Yesterday I went to buy a new pair of shoes. I tried on a lot of pairs. I was trying on a really nice pair when the shop assistant walked by. How are they she asked. I told her they were a little too tight. She said maybe you should try them with the tongue out. I did. I said, thath tho thood, theyrre thill thoo thigt.

HEY, KIDS!
I went to try out the new Computer Restaurant.
I ordered a hard drive from their menu.
When it came, it came with the instructions.
Must eat one byte at a time.

HEY, KIDS!
I can never get it right. Grandma said to me, is it just me or is the dog getting fatter? Apparently, it's not just you, isn't the right answer.

HEY, KIDS!
Grandma told me she believes all our children and all our grandchildren were spoiled when they were little.
I just thought all kids smelled that way.

HEY, KIDS!
Many years ago when I loved to run, I went overseas and entered a marathon in Northern Sweden.
I think I got lost and only realized it when
I crossed the Finnish line.

HEY, KIDS!
Grandma and I went shopping for a new lounge suite. The salesman told us that the one we really liked will sit five people without problems.
We didn't buy it because after considering our family and friends we realised we couldn't
find five people without problems.

HEY, KIDS!
I had to go to the doctor because I was bitten by a wolf.
Where the doctor asked.
I told him no, it was just an ordinary one.

HEY, KIDS!
I can remember when I got my first pure bread dog. He wasn't much fun he just loafed around all day.
I thought he may have had a yeast infection but I had no dough left over to pay for a vet.
When I first got him, I thought he was the greatest thing since sliced bread but he was so kneady.
I couldn't get him to rise in the morning and I remember thinking if he doesn't smarten up,
he'll be toast.

HEY, KIDS!
I was cleaning up my computer getting rid of any viruses. A mate of mine gave me a good tip to do it with the lights off. He told me that the light attracts more bugs, so it is best to work in the dark.

HEY, KIDS!
You know if we are really serious about saving our planet, we should destroy all calendars. They're the main reason why our days are numbered.

HEY, KIDS!
I hired a man to go buy my fruit for me now that I'm getting older. I fired him today. I hate to let the Mango but he was driving me bananas.

HEY, KIDS!
Grandma put me on a gluten free diet because of my constant bad headaches. It worked.
She was right, clearly my grains were the problem.

HEY, KIDS!
The last time Grandma and I went to the zoo we were rather disappointed with the number of animals on display. That is, except for the Bison. There was this massive herd of Bison all gathered in one corner of a large enclosure down the back. I asked one of the zoo keepers who was working nearby why there were so many Bison. He said we were witnessing a very rare event that occurs only every two hundred years.
He said it was the bison tennial.

HEY, KIDS!
Do you realise that it doesn't really matter if you are tall or short, thin or carrying a bit of weight, rich or poor, outgoing or an introvert, at the end of the day, it's night.

HEY, KIDS!
A long time ago I had a friend named Jack.
I always remember Jack because he had a very special
talent. Jack could communicate with vegetables.
That's right. Jack and the beans talk.

HEY, KIDS!
Years ago I took my kids to the zoo. A week later I went
back to see how they had settled in.

HEY, KIDS!
Grandma told me to take a spider out rather than kill it.
I was okay with that. We went for coffee and cake.
Nice spider. He said that he was a web developer.

HEY, KIDS!
According to Grandma all Grandad jokes have to be
written down on paper. I asked why I just can't text
them like I always do.
She said it's not a Grandad joke unless it's tearable.

HEY, KIDS!
Last time I went to America a cocky customs officer
asked me where I would be visiting. I told him San Jose.
He laughed and said it is pronounced San Hosey. Here
in America, we pronounce our J's as H.
Now how long will you be staying?
Oh, I replied. I will be here from Hanuary
right through to Hune or Huly.

HEY, KIDS!
I just got a message from my Barber informing me that
he will not be cutting hair any longer. He said that from
now on he will be only cutting it shorter.

HEY, KIDS!
The teachers in the old days were really tough and mean. I remember a teacher pointing a ruler at me and saying "at the end of this ruler is an idiot".
I got the strap for asking "which end?"

HEY, KIDS!
I was telling Grandma that one of my old friends fell off his motor bike. I told her that he had brain damage, 2 broken arms and is blind in one eye.
She said, no wonder he fell off, no one should be riding a bike in that condition.

HEY, KIDS!
I've been wanting to lose a bit of weight. I was looking at a diet book that was claiming that I could return to my original weight in just 30 days.
I didn't buy it, 6lb 3 ounces is just not realistic.

HEY, KIDS!
Everyone should watch the ABC. I just watched a documentary about beavers, it's the best dam show I have ever seen.

HEY, KIDS!
A so-called farmer friend suggested I put horse manure on my strawberries. I'm never doing that again.
I'm going back to cream.

HEY, KIDS!
Did you know that Grandma treats me like a God.
It's true. It's like I don't exist until she wants something.

HEY, KIDS!
Most of my life I have found it difficult to make big decisions. Grandma has always said that I'm indecisive. But I'm not so sure.

HEY, KIDS!
I was so hungry yesterday that I ate a clock. It took a while to go down as it was very time consuming and even more so when I went back for seconds.

HEY, KIDS!
During the Covid lockdown I witnessed one of our neighbours kicking his own front door in. When I asked him what he was doing, he explained that he was a professional thief and because of the pandemic he had to work from home.

HEY, KIDS!
When I was a teacher, I loved to be called Sir.
I went by a different name when I was on yard duty.
I was known as Sir Veillance.
Gee I'm funny.

HEY, KIDS!
According to Grandma there is no dinner tonight. She made nothing last night either. When I asked why, she explained that when she prepared, she had made enough to last two nights.

HEY, KIDS!
Grandma went to the doctor recently because she had a blocked ear. The doctor asked her to describe the symptoms. I was surprised when she answered, "Homer is the big dude and Marge is the one with the blue hair.' She really did have a blocked ear.

HEY, KIDS!
There are a lot of things I don't know. Like I didn't know that buffalos had wings. They do. I had some at a restaurant the other night. Strange though, they taste a lot like chicken.

HEY, KIDS!
English is a wonderful language. However, I really hate it when I read read as read and not read, so I then have to re-read read as read so I can read read correctly before it makes any sense.

HEY, KIDS!
I decided I would go and stand outside for a day. After a while, Grandma asked me what I was doing. I told her, if anyone asks about me she can truthfully tell them, I am outstanding. I am.

HEY, KIDS!
Another interesting fact I stumbled across. The difference between a literalist and a kleptomaniac is just a comma. Because, a literalist takes things literally and a kleptomaniac takes things, literally.

HEY, KIDS!
When we first got the new car Grandma couldn't get it to go at night. She could drive it fine in the day time but it just wouldn't go for her at night. We ended up calling the dealership and they checked it over. They found nothing wrong. But it was still the same for her, it would go in the day but she couldn't get it to go at night. In the end I decided to go with her to see what she was doing. I asked her if she understood how the car works with all the modern equipment. She was offended and clearly informed me that she was not stupid. She said I put the stick in D for the day and N for the night. What hope have I got?

HEY, KIDS!
Many years ago I had a girl friend who had a severe limp. Actually, one of her legs was shorter than the other. But what was really funny was that her name was Eileen. Really, it's true.

HEY, KIDS!
My neighbour just bought a new electric Honda Civic. For some reason he can't work out how to charge it. I think he now regrets not buying the Honda Accord.

HEY, KIDS!
Grandma called out to me while I was in the bathroom. "Did you try the new shampoo that I bought you?" I answered, "no, I noticed it was for dry hair and I just wet mine".

HEY, KIDS!
This morning I went to a Pentecostal church and went to the front to ask the Pastor to pray for my hearing. He immediately placed one hand on my head and the other over my ear. He started shaking me and trying to push me over, all the time speaking in a strange tongue. After about a minute he stopped and asked me how my hearing was.
I told him I don't know, it's not until Tuesday.

HEY, KIDS!
On our bike ride yesterday Grandma and I rode down a very interesting street. All the houses were numbered with numbers like 64k, 128k, 256k, 512k, and 1MB. When I looked at the street sign, I realized that we had just taken a trip down memory lane.

HEY, KIDS!
Now I am growing old things don't work as they used to. Yesterday I called the incontinence hotline. The person answered, can you hold please. I shouted into the phone. No, that's why I'm calling.

HEY, KIDS!
When I was young, I had a very busy life. On Tuesdays after school, I would go to book club with Miss Reid. Tuesday lunch I would do writing with Miss Print. Saturday morning, I would go with Miss Sing for a music lesson. And Saturday afternoon I would go learn Chinese with Miss Pronounce.

HEY, KIDS!
I always remember Wednesday afternoons at school. In Legal Studies I had Miss Represent and Miss Trial. They were fun times. And I also had this very old Communications teacher Miss Dial. And then there was this young teacher who would wear very short skirts and revealing outfits. If I remember correctly, I think her name was Miss Appropriate.

HEY, KIDS!
I never studied Politics at school but you will never guess the name of the teacher who taught it. That's right it was Miss Govern. We also had a teacher that would run fundraising in the school for special charities, Miss Giving. Unfortunately, one year some money went missing so we started referring to her as Miss Take or Miss Took.

HEY, KIDS!

When I was at school Miss Fitt was always a very community minded teacher. She was a PE teacher but also volunteered to run the second-hand uniform shop. Outside school she was the President of the Epilepsy Foundation and at lunchtime she would organize a friendship club for all the other Miss Fitts in the school like me.

HEY, KIDS!

At school we had this sex education teacher who was a bit weird. Miss Conceive. And there was this other teacher Miss Alliance who got sacked because they reckon she wasn't cut out for teaching.
I had to do special math tutoring once a week with Miss Calculate and she made nearly as many mistakes as I did.

HEY, KIDS!

In Primary school I was sent to see Miss Understand the school psychologist, I actually found out that her real name was Miss Understanding and she was an expert in conflict management. Any way she gave me some tests and diagnosed me with dyslexia. So, then I was referred to Miss Spelt and Miss Order for tutoring.

HEY, KIDS!

When I went to secondary school things were not good. The teacher who placed us in classes was Miss Inform. I thought this was rather funny as she was also the careers advisor. Anyway, I was not happy when I found out that I was in Miss Fortune's home room and Miss Judge was my Coordinator.

And, I had this really annoying English teacher who would always interrupt me and correct my sentences. She would often change my words to say something very different to what I was trying to say. I can't quite remember her name; yes I can, it was Miss Constrew.

Half way through the year we changed English teachers. Then I had Miss Quote who wasn't much better.

Then there was Miss Place who was always losing my work. And Miss Treat who was the meanest teacher in the school. She always seemed a lot nicer when she was on canteen duty. And I will never forget Miss Ille who was always going off at someone.

I can also remember this weird teacher I had for horticulture Miss Tree. I could never work her out. And I can remember having the saddest teacher ever. She never smiled Miss Ery.

My year 8 home group teacher would never call my name correctly. She would always say FINDLAAY. You won't believe it but her name was Miss Pronounce. We also had a teacher who could teach all subjects. It didn't matter what subject it was she would teach it. Her name was Miss Cellanious.

HEY, KIDS!

When I first went to secondary school there were these four teachers who really gave me the creeps. Fortunately, they never taught me. They were always together, always wearing black, all had black hair and black painted eyes. When they looked at you, you felt like you were being cursed. Miss Terrious, Miss Tick , Miss Tify and Miss Tique. It makes me shiver just to remember them. One day I saw them coming. I ran, tripped over, grazed my knee and ended up with Miss Adventure in the sickbay.

HEY, KIDS!

At school I had this teacher who thought she was funny. She was always playing stupid little tricks on everyone. Miss Chief was her name. And, there was this one teacher who seemed to hate every other female teacher in the school. Miss Ogyny. And Miss Ogamy was an activist who was openly against people getting married.

HEY, KIDS!
My doctor just told me that I have a narcissistic personality disorder. He is an idiot. He doesn't know what he's talking about. I am one of the smartest men in the world so I would have worked it out well before him. Maybe he should give up medicine and do something that better suits his abilities.

HEY, KIDS!
I'm sure my glasses were talking to me yesterday. I kept hearing this voice. You are not wearing the right shoes. That doesn't go there. You can't say that. At first, I thought it was Grandma, but in the end I realised that it was my corrective lenses.

HEY, KIDS!
I just got shot by a man with an evaporating gun. One way or another I will be mist.

HEY, KIDS!
Grandma got booked by the police yesterday. She was not happy. In fact she became quite argumentative. She is still insisting that it's impossible to do 100 kilometres per hour when she had only been driving for 3 minutes.

HEY, KIDS!
When I was a teacher, I loved being called Sir. It always reminded me of my sailing days when I was addressed as Sir Cumnavigate.

HEY, KIDS!
Yesterday I told you how I loved being referred to as Sir. It makes me feel like I am respected. It has caused me to think back to the many times that I have been called Sir.

There was the time when I was a JP and was referred to as Sir Tify.

Then there was the time I was a butcher and was addressed as Sir Loin. But the most memorable was back in my teaching days. It was my birthday. I walked into a very quiet classroom and was welcomed as Sir Prize. Oh yes, the time I did some Knight work for a local Land Developer. They called me Sir Veyor.

HEY, KIDS!
My school once needed to declare a number of teachers in excess. I was worried that I would become Sir Plus.

They asked for teachers to volunteer but there was no way I was going to be Sir Render. In the end the school targeted a language teacher of Chinese who was always angry. He was known as Sir Lee.

HEY, KIDS!
I once considered becoming a doctor because I liked the title Sir John. Then someone pointed out that I might get called Sir Jerry or Sir Jickle and that didn't sound quite so regal. So, I gave up on the idea.

HEY, KIDS!
I once had a job on the gate at the zoo. They called me Sir Curity. I kept watching the animals so they transferred me to feed the snakes.
There I was given a very regal double title.
I was known as Sir Vant of Sir Pent.

HEY, KIDS!
There was the time when I was a teenager that I did some work for an electrician. The boss used to call me Little Sir Cut.

I can remember it because I would leave there and go straight to into delivering pamphlets where I would become Sir Culate. Luckily, I was never a clown or I might have been called Sir Cus.

HEY, KIDS!
I have been shown so much respect. Even the law has shown me great respect. They didn't call me Sir but they did refer to me as Mister. I was at court and the policeman referred to me as Mr. Meanner.

HEY, KIDS!
I have been going through my old school things and I came across the staff list of my Secondary School.

Miss Demeanor. Principal.

Miss Chiefly. Ass Principal.

Miss Govern. Business Manager.

Miss Reading. English

Miss Spelling. English

Miss Organised. Office Administrator

Miss Giving. Special Projects Organiser.

Miss Appropriately. Uniform and Dress Code.

Miss Shapely. Art and Design.

Miss Chevious. Student Management.

Miss Layed. Lost Property.

Miss Represent. Student Advocate.

Miss Print. Art

Miss Pronounce. Language.

Miss Happ. Sickbay

Miss Informed. Careers

Miss Fitt. PE. & Social Club.
Miss Engage. Student Relations.
Miss Sing. Music & Lost Property
Miss Conceive. Health & Human Development.
Miss Calculate. Maths.
Miss Used. Second Hand Uniform.
Miss Judge. Legal Studies
Miss Quote. Debating.
Miss Treated. Student Discipline.
Miss Understood. History.
Miss Pronounced. Speech Therapist.
Miss Inform. Newsletter.
Miss Tified. Science and Philosophy
Miss Firing. Clay modelling.

HEY, KIDS!

In my last year at school I thought I might do Accounting as an elective with Miss Spent. Considering my maths skills, it was not a good use of my time. O my misspent youth. So, I changed to Philosophy with Miss Tified. The subject was strange and weird and hard to grasp but I liked the teacher. She always made me laugh. In the end I ended up doing Horticulture with Miss Altow. I'd had her before as she was also a music teacher. I had her for choir.

HEY, KIDS!

If I'm not Miss Taken, and I'm not, I left school. My journey out was a difficult path to navigate. Miss It was the teacher in charge of absences so I had a lot to do with her over the years. I had a meeting with Miss Using who pointed out that I was not making good use of my time at school. The school arranged a meeting for me with Miss Place the Careers Teacher. Miss Printed gave me my leaving certificate which had my name spelt wrong so I had to take it back to Miss Take to get it fixed.

HEY, KIDS!
You will be happy to know that I finally left school. My first job was in a church in the city. Because I was musical, I got a job at St. Paul's as a Bell Ringer.
I didn't do much in my first week they were really just showing me the ropes.

HEY, KIDS!
I just bought a new Toilet brush. I wouldn't recommend it, I'm going back to paper.

HEY, KIDS!
I stopped at a petrol station to put some air in my Tyres. They charged me $1.50 for air. Of course, I went in to complain. The attendant just looked at me and said "that's inflation for you".

HEY, KIDS!
Grandma said to me. "You have absolutely no sense of direction". I have absolutely no idea where that came from.

HEY, KIDS!
I was talking to the manager of the local supermarket. He is an extremely smart and intelligent man. I asked him how he became so smart. He told me that it was from eating fish heads. We have some on special for $4 each he told me. I bought some. They were disgusting and nearly made me sick. A week later I wasn't any smarter and was back at the supermarket talking to the manager. You haven't eaten enough the manager said.

So, I bought another 40. After another week went by and a few trips to the doctors, I went back rather angry and annoyed. I found the manager and pointed out that he was ripping me off because I was paying $4 for a fish head and I could buy the whole fish for $2. "You see," he said, "you are getting smarter already".

HEY, KIDS!

I saw a man get hit by a car the other day. I stopped to help. I called 000. The operator asked me where I was. I told her that I was on Eucalyptus Street.
She asked me to spell it. I hesitated before telling her that I would drag him over to Pine St and call her back.

HEY, KIDS!

I have just realised that the Royal System is far from fair and equitable.

King Charles has been assigned a King bed.

Camilla, Queen Consort has been assigned a Queen bed.

Prince William has only been assigned an Heir bed.

HEY, KIDS!

I asked an overseas friend what is the best thing about living in Switzerland?

She said she didn't really know but the flag is a big plus.

HEY, KIDS!

Someone told me that childbirth is the most painful experience ever.
Maybe I was too young to remember but I don't think it hurt that much.

HEY, KIDS!
I've got some good news and some bad news. The bad news is that I took the wrong medication this morning. The good news is that I am now protected from worms and fleas for the next 3 months.

HEY, KIDS!
I was driving in the country recently and passed a little country store. It had a sign on the front.

FLOWERS

PRODUCE

EGGS

Boy they're weird in the country, everyone knows that they don't.

HEY, KIDS!
Did you know that my 3 favourite things are eating my family and not using commas.

HEY, KIDS!
I told Grandma that I need a date for a Halloween party. Do you know what she said. October 31st.

HEY, KIDS!
I have wondered why nurses always carry red pens. Do you know? It's in case they are called on to draw blood.

HEY, KIDS!
My brother David has had his ID stolen. Now I just call him Dav.

HEY, KIDS!
When I was studying Geography at school I would always think of Europe as being a big frying pan.
Do you know why?
It is because it has Greece at the bottom.

HEY, KIDS!
I recently met a man who was living in an inflated tube and tyre. I thought I would help him out so I hammered a nail into the tyre. Now he lives in a flat.

HEY, KIDS!
I once was granted one wish for my birthday from a Genie. I thought I was clever when I wished "I wish I was you". The Genie said "that's weurd but alrught. Have a nuce day and happy burthday."

HEY, KIDS!
I offered to mow my new neighbour's lawn if he would let me have a ride in his new elevator.
I think he is going to take me up on it.

HEY, KIDS!
My computer was playing up. It was jumping all over the place. It was behaving so stupid like it was drunk. I called geeks on line and they fixed it very quickly.
They said it was too many screen shots.

HEY, KIDS!
Grandma and I went out for lunch. We were reading over the menu when I sensed that something was wrong. "Are you alright" I asked her. "No", she said "I am not alright." "What's wrong?" I asked.

"For starters, I am sick of your stupid jokes." "Okay" I said, "and what would you like for the main course?"

HEY, KIDS!
You know some people can be so rude. I was sitting in a restaurant just about to bite into a delicious steak when a lady walked by with a stacked plate of salad. She looked at me and said, "do you know an animal died so you can eat that steak?"
I looked at her plate and replied.
"He might not have died if you didn't eat all his food ".

HEY, KIDS!
My new neighbour has a great sense of humour. She told me she has been married 4 times. Her first husband was a Banker. Her second husband was a Clown in a circus. Her third husband was a Preacher and now she is married to an Undertaker. "That's quite a variety" I said to her. She replied "One for the money, two for the show, three to get ready and four to go."

HEY, KIDS!
I'm a bit bored so I have decided to do an experiment. I have ordered a chicken and an egg from Amazon.

I'll let you know.

HEY, KIDS!
I once had a girl friend who was an Optician.
I didn't really like her that much and I tried five times to break up with her. Every time I told her that I couldn't see her anymore she would move closer and say "how about now?"

HEY, KIDS!
When I first met your Grandma she was wearing this strange white suit with this helmet thing covering her whole head. She was covered in bee stings and she smelt like honey. That's when I knew she was a keeper.

HEY, KIDS!
You won't believe it. Someone just called me,
sneezed in the phone and hung up.
I am really getting sick of these cold calls.

HEY, KIDS!
Being a retired teacher, I can get quite pedantic about
spelling and punctuation. I was walking past a farm the
other day and there was a sign that said "Duck, eggs". I
was thinking, there is no need for the comma.
And then it hit me.

HEY, KIDS!
Yesterday I spent 2 hours trying to solve a problem.
Someone left an envelope at my front door clearly
marked DO NOT BEND. I finally worked it out. I got
Grandma to pick it up.

HEY, KIDS!
Some thief broke into my house and stole my fruit.
I'm lost for words, I don't know what to say,
I'm actually peachless.

HEY, KIDS!
I just read that there are no fish in Egypt,
but I think they are in de Nile

HEY, KIDS!
My friend Rod and I decided to start a new business
doing night tours in old cemeteries. We have hired 3
tour guides to work for us. Last night was my first time
on a tour. I have to admit that I was very scared at first.
Then I remembered, even though I walk through the
valley of the shadow of death I will fear no evil,
for my Rod and my Staff will comfort me.

HEY, KIDS!
My parents were always telling me that money doesn't grow on trees. I spent the last 50 years not believing them because all the banks I've seen have branches.

HEY, KIDS!
When I was at school, one day I was worried that I might be in trouble for something I didn't do. I thought it best to speak to my teacher first.
"Miss Lead, can I get in trouble for something I didn't do.?" "Of course not, that would be unfair."
"Good," I said, "because I didn't do my homework."
Clever boy.

HEY, KIDS!
I have met our new neighbour about 5 times now and every time she acts as if we haven't met before.
It happened again today and she didn't know me.
The funny thing is her name is Dee. Dee Mentia.

HEY, KIDS!
Not long ago, Grandma was arrested for stealing a can of peaches. She had to go to court. The judge asked her why she did it. Grandma said that she was hungry.
I think the judge felt sorry for her. I think that he wanted to go easy on her because he asked how many peaches were in the tin. Six, Grandma replied. Okay then I sentence you to 6 days in jail,
said the judge. It was at this point that I felt that I needed to say something.

The judge asked me if it was important. I told him I believe it was very important. "Okay what is it?" he said. "Your honour, I need to tell you that she also stole a can of peas."

HEY, KIDS!
Grandma got out another 1000 piece jigsaw puzzle and was upset because there was one piece missing.
I got out my one and only jigsaw puzzle and I wasn't upset when I found that I had 999 pieces missing.
I don't understand some people.

HEY, KIDS!
Grandma is thinking about getting me a camouflage jacket for Christmas. The trouble is that I can't see myself wearing it.

HEY, KIDS!
An English man, an Australian and an Irish man are waiting to get into Heaven. At the gate St Peter says to them, in order to get in at this time of year you need to provide something that says something about the Christmas story. The English man gets out his lighter and makes a flame. This is a Christmas candle he says.
Okay not good but just good enough to get you in.
The Australian gets out a set of keys and starts shaking them. These are Christmas bells he says.
St Peter is not really impressed but lets him pass.
The Irishman goes to his pockets and pulls out a pair of ladies' underwear. Hold on a minute says St Peter.
How do these represent the Christmas story.
The Irish man replies, these are Carols.

HEY, KIDS!
Grandma asked me if I could speak any other languages. I told her that I knew a little German.

She's about 5 feet 4 and is currently living in Switzerland.

HEY, KIDS!
Grandma asked me what do you call a construction worker who falls off a roof?

An ambulance, I told her.

HEY, KIDS!
Grandma was looking over my old resume. Grandma looks at me and says "you have written here that you are quick at mathematics, what's 17x26?" "92" I said. "That's not even close." I replied,
"Maybe not, but it was quick."

HEY, KIDS!
Grandma and I are considering buying YouTube, Twitter and Facebook. If we do, we will merge them into one company. We will call it, Youtwitface.

HEY, KIDS!
I have been remembering a conversation I had with my dad many years ago. I had auditioned for a school play and got the part as a man married for 25 years.
Dad was so proud and encouraging.
He said "Well done son, hang in there, next year you might graduate to a speaking part."

HEY, KIDS!
Grandma and I have bought a new pet. It's a termite. He is very cute. We are going to call him Clint.

Clint Eatswood.

HEY, KIDS!
I asked Grandma what the difference is between Ignorance and arrogance. She replied.

"I don't know and I don't care ".
Maybe you can help me?

HEY, KIDS!
Halloween is the perfect time for zombies to come out.
We had one banging on our door last night yelling
"I'm gay".

HEY, KIDS!
I thought that I should have a talk to Grandma about
a rather sensitive issue. I told her that I thought her
underwear was too tight and too revealing.
Do you know what she said.
She told me if I didn't like them to wear my own.

HEY, KIDS!
I am planning ahead for my next birthday. I asked
Grandma how much it would cost to buy a large singing
group. She said, "a choir". Okay. How much will it cost
to acquire a large singing group. I always get it wrong.

HEY, KIDS!
Grandma has had a bad cough all week and has not
been well at all. I have had to remind her that it's not
the cough that carries you off it's the coffin
they carry you off in.

HEY, KIDS!
Did you know that if you buy someone a plane ticket
they will fly for a day. However, if you push someone
out of a plane they will fly for the rest of their life.

HEY, KIDS!
When we were overseas, I can remember a time when
we were at an airport collecting our luggage when
Grandma fainted and fell on the luggage travelator.
A few people standing around were rather concerned
but I knew if we were patient she would
come around eventually.

HEY, KIDS!
Trav and Brad are both bald. I suggest that we draw a couple of rabbits on their heads. It has been discovered that from a distance they look like hairs.

HEY, KIDS!
Two years ago Grandma and I decided to join a support group for antisocial people.
We haven't met yet.

HEY, KIDS!
Grandma was trying to encourage me, build me up and make me feel better. She said "In those times when you feel really down and you hate yourself,
just realise you're not alone.
There are many others who hate you too."

HEY, KIDS!
Before Grandma and I got married we had to go to some marriage preparation classes. In one of the sessions the counsellor said that he thought I had a fear of getting married. He asked me if I knew what the symptoms were. "I can't say I do," I said.
"Yep, that's one of them"

HEY, KIDS!
Yesterday we had a miracle occur right next door. They had a blind builder working on their pergola. You know what happened. The builder picked up his hammer and saw. It was a miracle.

HEY, KIDS!
We have just had another miracle. A deaf man was chasing sheep in the paddock at the end of our street.
He gathered his flock and herd.
This is amazing.

HEY, KIDS!
Didn't you know that I can always tell when you are lying. That's not all, I can also tell when you are standing or sitting.

HEY, KIDS!
I just took up a new sport. Yep, blindfolded archery. It's really great. You all should try it. You don't know what you're missing.

HEY, KIDS!
When I tested positive to the Coronavirus I went to the chemist. I found this lady and asked her what kills the Coronavirus? She said Amonia Cleaner. I apologised and explained that I thought she worked there.

HEY, KIDS!
Medical experts in China have just released the name of the first person to catch Coronavirus.
His name is Ah Choo.

They have stated that they don't think it will last long because most things made in China don't.

HEY, KIDS!
I have just read that no one in Antarctica has caught Coronavirus. Apparently, it's because they are ice-o-lated.

HEY, KIDS!
You know I was thinking. In 2036 all the babies born in 2020-2022 will be known as quarantineens.

HEY, KIDS!
I have been thinking a lot about Covid. I was wondering what the difference is between the Alpha and Delta variant. I have no idea, it's all Greek to me.

HEY, KIDS!
Knock knock. Who's there? Etch. Etch-who.
That's right it's Grandma with Coronavirus.

HEY, KIDS!
I just got arrested at Woolworths. Now that I am allowed out again, I rang the Coronavirus hotline for advice. They told me that to go to the supermarket I only had to wear a mask. Apparently, the police don't agree. Please send money for bail.

HEY, KIDS!
Grandma and I went out to dinner last night.
At the end of the meal the waiter came over and asked me "do you wanna box for your left-over food"?
I told him no, I am anti-violent, and if it means so much to you, you can have it.

HEY, KIDS!
Last time I went to America I visited the White House. I needed to go to the bathroom so I found a toilet down a small passage way. I was stopped by a security guard who told me that I can't go in there,
it's for Biden.

HEY, KIDS!
When my first child was born the doctor asked me if I had ever been present for a birth before. I told him yes but only once. He asked how it was for me. I told him that I remember it being very dark then suddenly there was bright light. I don't remember much more.

HEY, KIDS!
Yesterday Grandma told me that she is losing her mind. I told her that I know why that is.
It's because she has been giving me a piece of it every day for the last 47 years. Can't be much left now.

HEY, KIDS!
I received an email yesterday explaining how reading maps backwards is a more efficient way to plan your travel. It was telling me to start at my destination and work backwards.
After looking at it very closely I finally realized that it was just spam.

HEY, KIDS!
I broke my glasses yesterday and you'll never guess who I bumped into on my way to the optometrist to get them fixed. That's right, everyone.

HEY, KIDS!
Just before Christmas I received this rather strange email. It said "Now the year is coming to an end I urge you to stay safe and take extra care of yourself. Avoid accidents at all costs. This is because spare parts for older models like you are no longer stocked or available. Take care." Who sent this?

HEY, KIDS!
Grandma and I received this message in the post yesterday. It is supposed to be a Christmas card.

Dear Grandparents,

ABCDEFGHIJKMNOPQRSTUVWXYZ

Could someone please explain how this is a Christmas card? No L.

HEY, KIDS!
Now that I am getting older my body is failing me.
I think the most reliable part of my body are my fingers. I can always count on them.

HEY, KIDS!
Grandma walked into our home office when I was standing naked facing the computer screen. Grandma read what was on the screen and said,
"this is not how to prove you're not a robot."

HEY, KIDS!
I have asked Santa for a new birthday suit this year. The one I have is old and wrinkled.

HEY, KIDS!
I heard Grandma screaming out from the bathroom. "You left the toilet seat up again." I went to investigate. Grandma was standing there in the bathroom, red faced, yelling something about the seat being left up.
"I fell in," Grandma said.
I replied, "I know, I heard the splash and I came running as quickly as I could to flush it."

HEY, KIDS!
A new supermarket has opened up near our house. It is very modern. It has an automatic water mister to keep the produce fresh. Just before it goes on, you can hear the sound of distant thunder and the smell of fresh rain.

When you approach the milk section, you can hear cows mooing and get the scent of fresh hay. When you get near the egg section you can hear the sound of hens clucking and the air is filled with the aroma of bacon and eggs frying. The veggie department features the smell of fresh buttered corn. I won't go anywhere near the toilet paper section in that store.

HEY, KIDS!
Grandma never stops nagging me because I never put the toilet seat down. You know I think I will.
I am a bit tired of carrying it around with me anyway.

HEY, KIDS!
This man was driving down a road when he runs over a rabbit. The man stops and goes to assist the poor rabbit. The rabbit is obviously dead. Another driver stops to see what is going on. When the helper sees what has happened, he runs to his car and brings out an aerosol can. The man approaches the dead rabbit and sprays the aerosol all over the rabbit. The rabbit suddenly wakes up and jumps to his feet. The restored rabbit runs a few steps down the road and stops, turns around and waves. He then runs another few steps down the road, stops, turns around and waves. The rabbit keeps repeating this as he continues his journey down the road until he is out of sight. The man who hit the rabbit looks at the helper amazed at what he has just seen. What is in that can he asks?
He then takes the can and reads the label.

It reads, Hair restorer with permanent wave.

HEY, KIDS!
Sylvester Stallone said he wants to make a movie about classical music.
He says, "I'll be Beethoven." Jean Claude Van Damme says "okay, I'll be Mozart" and
Arnold Schwarzenegger says "I'll be Bach."

HEY, KIDS!
When I was younger, I thought Jesus' family name was Fish. My mother asked me why.
I told her that it had to be Fish because his dad's name was Joe Fish.

HEY, KIDS!
Today Grandma and I went for a drive to explore some old places that we haven't seen in many years.
One of the places we wanted to visit again we couldn't find on the map. In the end we decided to have a look in an area call Memouf. And you know what we found.
That's right we found Metung. Beautiful place.

HEY, KIDS!
The other night I was feeling a bit upset with Grandma. Grandma asked me what was wrong. I told her that for the last 47 years all she has done is find mistakes in everything I say. Grandma responded,
"that would be 48 years dear."

HEY, KIDS!
A few years ago Grandma and I were using a laundry in New York to wash our travelling clothes. While our clothes were being washed, we looked up and saw a sign on the wall. The sign said, when you have finished washing, please remove all your clothes. I looked at Grandma and said, ladies first.

HEY, KIDS!
Grandma and I are considering not wearing our glasses anymore. Yes, I think we've seen enough.

HEY, KIDS!
When I was young, I considered many different career paths. At one time I even considered scuba diving. However, deep down I knew it wasn't for me.

HEY, KIDS!
Have you heard about the 4 constipated men in the Bible. First there was Cain. He wasn't Able. Then there was Moses. He had to take 2 tablets. Then there was

Solomon. The Bible says he sat on the throne for 40 years. And lastly, there was David. He wrote that there was nothing in Heaven or Earth that could move him.

HEY, KIDS!
Years ago I needed to speak to one of my teenage daughters about her attitude. She looked at me in the eye and said "for complaints about attitude please speak to the manufacturer".

HEY, KIDS!
While I am in quarantine, I have run out of toilet paper. Yesterday I had to use lettuce, today is the tip of the iceberg, tomorrow remains to be seen.

HEY, KIDS!
One time when my son was growing up, he told me that he wanted to be a politician. I said "Are you mad? Are you stupid? Are you insane?"

He immediately changed his mind. "Forget it" he said, "there appears to be too many requirements."

HEY, KIDS!
I have just realised that the relationship between Grandma and I is mostly psychological. It's true. One of us is psycho and the other is logical. I wonder which one? Ha ha ha.

HEY, KIDS!
Hello my name is Improvement. I went for an overnight stay in a Motel. I didn't bother booking because I believed that I didn't need to. The Hotel manager said that they didn't have a room. I told him that there had to be a room because my mother always told me, there is always room for improvement.

HEY, KIDS!
Grandma traumatically ripped the blankets off me last night. Don't worry I will recover.

HEY, KIDS!
I was home alone and decided to take a relaxing warm bath. I had the lights turned down low and a candle burning. I was nearly asleep. It was then it happened. I was so scared I nearly jumped out of the bath. I couldn't see anything and then it happened again. A tap on my shoulder.

HEY, KIDS!
I was on the train going to the city and this man got on and sat down beside me. I was looking at a picture of Grandma on my phone. He asked, "is she your wife?" My response, "she's beautiful isn't she?" "You should see my wife" he responded. "Why? is she beautiful as well?" "No," he said, "she's an optician."

HEY, KIDS!
Grandma just came in and told me she had blisters on her hands from the broom. That's easy fixed I told her. Take the car next time.

HEY, KIDS!
After an hour and a half, I phoned the shop. I asked "will my pizza be long?" "No," he said, "it will be round."

HEY, KIDS!
Yesterday Grandma asked me to describe her. I had to really think hard. In the end I said ABCDEFGHIJK. What is that supposed to mean she asked. Adorable, Beautiful, Cute, Delightful, Elegant, Fantastic, Gorgeous and Honourable, I told her. She seemed to be happy with my answer. Then she asked. What about the IJK. I'm just kidding.

HEY, KIDS!
Yesterday Grandma told me that she read an article about the dangers of drinking too much. Apparently, it bothered her so much that she decided never to read again.

HEY, KIDS!
Someone told Grandma that bathing in milk is very good for your skin. So, she ordered 1000 litres of milk to be delivered to our home. She ordered it straight from the dairy and before they delivered it, they rang to confirm the order. I answered the phone "Did you order 1000 litres of milk?" I called out to Grandma, "did you order 1000 litres of milk?" "Yes," she replied. "Yes, we did" I told the man on the phone. "Did you need it pasteurized?" he asked me. I called out to Grandma, "do you need it pasteurized?" "No" she said, "just up to my neck."

HEY, KIDS!
Grandma is getting weirder by the day. Yesterday I heard her talking to someone on the phone and telling them that some crocodiles can grow up to 15 feet. That's strange I thought every crocodile that I have seen has only had 4. Please advise.

HEY, KIDS!
I asked Grandma, our walking encyclopedia, how much room did I need to grow fungi? She replied "As mushroom as possible". I kill me!

HEY, KIDS!
The divorce court judge told Mr Clark that he had reviewed his case very carefully. "And," the judge said "I have decided to give your wife $775 a week." "That's very fair, your Honour" replied Mr Clark. "And every now and then I will try to chip in and send her a few dollars myself."

HEY, KIDS!
I have been pondering again. Too much time on my hands. I found a frog and started wondering where it came from. I mean where it really came from. So, I organized a DNA test. It turns out that the frog is part Australian, part English, part Italian and a tad-pole.

HEY, KIDS!
We once had a dentist friend at Church. The funny thing was his favourite hymn was Crown Him with many Crowns and His name was Dr I Pullum.

HEY, KIDS!
We have got a new neighbour. He is Irish and a bit strange. He never goes into the house. He just stays outside all day. His name is Patty, Patty O'Furniture.

HEY, KIDS!
Last Christmas Grandma told me that I was getting fat. In my defence I told her that I had had a lot on my plate recently. Now I am hungry. I should have remained silent.

HEY, KIDS!
Now I am officially old I have been thinking about my past. I can remember being at school. The teacher asked us, what do pig's give us? I put up my hand and said, bacon. Very good. What do sheep give us? I put my hand up again and said, wool. The teacher then asked us what does the big fat cow give us? I was quick to put my hand up again and said homework. Apparently, that wasn't the right answer.

HEY, KIDS!
A Priest was giving a children's talk in the Church. He asked the children, why do you think I wear this collar? One of the children put his hand up and yelled out, "because it kills fleas and Ticks up to 30 days".

HEY, KIDS!
I dreamt I died and went to Heaven. I was surprised that to get in I needed to answer three questions correctly. St Peter welcomed me and explained the test. The first question he asked was, How many days in a week start with the letter T?
I thought hard and answered two, today and tomorrow. St. Peter looked a little confused but couldn't say I was wrong. The second question was, how many seconds are there in a year?
I started counting on my fingers (and toes) and answered twelve. He looked confused again and asked how I came to this conclusion. I said the second of January, the second of February etc. again he had to pass me. The last question he asked was, what is God's first name? I quickly said, that's easy. It's Andy. Why do you think it's Andy? We used to sing about it in church all the time. Andy walks with me
Andy talks with me. Then I woke up singing.

HEY, KIDS!
I thought that I was doing well with my diet
but I must still look fat.
The first thing the shop attendant said to
me yesterday was "sorry about your weight".

HEY, KIDS!
If you are looking out for the Easter Bunny this year
just remember he is now old.
Maybe you should keep an eye out for
the old grey hare.

HEY, KIDS!
Do you know what's funny? I just saw a long line of rabbits, one following the other all heading into a burrow. The really funny thing is it made me think of a few members of our family.
Do you know why? It was a receding hare line.

HEY, KIDS!
For Easter this year I have decided to make an Easter Egg Roll. It's easy. You just put it on the bench and give it a little push.

HEY, KIDS!
I was on my way to the supermarket to get some food for Easter when I saw a rabbit run down a hole.
I stopped and poured some boiling water into the hole. To my surprise out hopped a Hot Cross Bun-ey.

HEY, KIDS!
The Irish Police have reported a cyclone that destroyed a Cemetery in Dublin. The police have reported uncovering over 1000 bodies so far and are expecting to find many more.

HEY, KIDS!
Grandma wanted a pair of crocodile shoes. She went into a shop and was surprised when she was told that they were over $2000. She refused to pay that and told the sales person that she would go and catch her own crocodile. The sales person laughed, explained that it was not that easy and wished her luck. Later that day the sales person was driving home past the local swamp and saw Grandma standing knee deep in the water holding a rifle. There was a large crocodile about 10 meters away heading straight towards her. Bang! The sales person stopped the car and ran over to Grandma shouting, what are you doing? Grandma

had shot the crocodile, grabbed it by the tail and had dragged it up onto the bank next to 6 others she had already shot. Grandma looked at the sales person and said, you know I think you might have been right. This is the 7th one I have caught and none of them are wearing shoes.

HEY, KIDS!
Grandma was in the Airport with two sacks over her shoulder when all of a sudden, she gets pulled over by Customs who started searching the sacks. They find that both sacks are full of mobile phones. The Customs officer asks Grandma, why do you have so many mobile phones? Grandma began to explain.
Well, she said, when I was overseas, I got a call from my husband back home who told me that he was starting up a jazz band, and could I bring back two saxophones, and here they are.

HEY, KIDS!
Many, many, many, many, years ago before we got married Grandma accidentally poked me in the eyes. The result was that I stopped seeing her for a while. O happy days.

HEY, KIDS!
Have you heard of Murphy's law? Murphy's law is the belief that if there is something that can go wrong, then it will go wrong. But have her heard of Cole's law? Cole's law is finely sliced cabbage and mayo. Ha Ha.

HEY, KIDS!
My old friend Joe has discovered the new Dolly Parton diet and it really works.
It made Joe lean, Joe lean, Joe lean, Joe lean.

HEY, KIDS!

My friend Harold was a painter who was trying to save money, so he decided to cut a few corners on his jobs. He won a contract to paint a church. To save some money he watered down the paint. Harold was just about finished the job and was standing high up on the scaffolding when there was this almighty clap of thunder and a lightning bolt. It started to pour and the rain washed all the paint from the walls. Harold fell and landed among the graves in the church yard. Harold knew this was a judgment from God and he went on his knees saying he was sorry for trying to rip off the church. "What can I do to make this right?"
He prayed. A booming voice echoed from the sky, "Repaint, repaint and thin no more."

HEY, KIDS!

Grandma once bought a pet parrot. Grandma was horrified to discover that all it did was say mean things to her and insult her. Nothing she did could stop it. Grandma was very worried because the whole family was coming over for Christmas dinner. However, when Christmas finally came, the parrot didn't say a word the entire time. After the meal and everyone had gone home the parrot said to Grandma. "Please forgive me for everything that I have said to you in the past, I am so, so sorry and I promise that I will never be rude to you again." "Wow" said Grandma "I am very glad to hear it." "If I may ask" said the parrot, "what on earth did that turkey say to you?"

HEY, KIDS!

I decided to write a memoir. Grandma came in and asked me what I was doing. I told her that I thought that it would be a shame not to put down on paper all the wisdom that I have acquired over my long lifetime. "So, how long do you think it will take to put all that wisdom down on paper? I want you to take me shopping" Grandma said. "I think I have finished" I told her. Grandma grabbed the paper and said, "well I am impressed, you've written nearly half a page."

HEY, KIDS!
Grandma just accused me of taking her Thesaurus again. I am dismayed, shocked, disturbed, extremely sad and disappointed, I am aghast and appalled that she could even think that I could do such a thing. What evidence, proof, facts, information could she possibly have for her to arrive at this conclusion, outcome, view, opinion or belief.
I just can't accept or come to terms with her conclusion, reasoned judgement, or final outcome.

HEY, KIDS!
Grandma was not very happy with yesterday's joke. She told me that she would make me eat my words. Now I have thesaurus throat.

HEY, KIDS!
Now Grandma can't find her dictionary. With her forgetting where she has put things, I'm starting to wonder what this means. I know. It's a word used to describe a thing, a place, a word to indicate a single object or idea. It is the singular of the word, these. I wonder how I know this!

HEY, KIDS!
Grandma really looks out for me. We were about to play a game of snooker when she asked me, "do you wanna break?" I told her I was alright to play for a while as we hadn't even started yet.

HEY, KIDS!
Throughout history Cleopatra is always described as being very beautiful. But, in reality that's only how Julius Caesar.

HEY, KIDS!
Years ago when I used to run, Grandma would always discourage people from sponsoring me in the marathon. She would tell everyone to be very careful because I have been known to take the money and run.

HEY, KIDS!
A mother bird and her baby were taking a long flight following a long highway. The baby bird said to his mum, "I haven't seen a windshield in ages'. The mother bird replied, "then you will just have to hold it".

HEY, KIDS!
Grandma suggested that I write a book instead of wasting my time with all these stupid puns and jokes. I thought, hey that's a novel idea.

HEY, KIDS!
Grandma just told me that the man who first invented knock knock jokes won the no bell prize.

HEY, KIDS!
I had a bad dream the other night. I dreamt that Grandma and I had gone on a holiday to Jerusalem. While we were there, Grandma died. I was told that I could bring Grandma back home for $10,000 or I could have her buried over there for $500.

I decided to have her brought home. I was asked why I would spend $10,000 to have her shipped home when she could be buried over there for just $500.
I told them that I knew of a man long, long, ago who died and was buried in Jerusalem. Then three days later he came back to life. I'm not prepared to take that chance. Then I woke up. Strange dream.

HEY, KIDS!

One of my neighbours asked me what was the secret to Grandma's and my happy marriage. I told him it all began just after we were married. Grandma and I were enjoying our honeymoon in the country and doing some horse riding. We had only travelled a short distance when Grandma's horse stepped in a hole and threw her off. Grandma stood up, walked over to the horse and said, "that's one".

A little further along Grandma's horse stumbled on a rock and almost threw her off again. Grandma lent over and said in the horse's ear, "that's two". Further on the horse tripped on a log and went down launching Grandma into some bushes. Grandma picked herself up out of the bushes reached into her saddle bag, took out a gun and shot the horse. I looked at Grandma and said, "darling what in the heck did you go and do that for?"
Grandma just looked at me and quietly said, "That's one." That was our first and last argument.

HEY, KIDS!

Grandma and I visited the National Art Gallery last week and I took my camera with me. I was talking to one of the attendants there and I asked him if I could take a picture. He was very nice and said that I could. However, the attendant at the door wasn't so nice. He took the picture off me and had me arrested.

HEY, KIDS!

Grandma and I went to an Italian restaurant last week. We had only just arrived when the owner came over and said "Sorry, sorry, no food today. My chef he just pasta way. I cannoli do so much. I so sorry my chef he now just a pizza history."

HEY, KIDS!

Grandma and I were having a very quiet afternoon sitting in a park outside a flower show. I bet Grandma $10 to strip off and run naked through the flower show. It's unlike Grandma but she took me up on it. A few minutes later Grandma streaked through the front door of the flower show. Then I hear this almighty roar and applause. A few minutes later Grandma comes back out wearing nothing but a sash. I asked, what happened in there? She said," I just won first prize for the best dried flower arrangement."

HEY, KIDS!

A long time ago I had an accident that resulted in me losing three of my fingers. I remember talking to the doctor asking if I will ever be able to write
with that hand again.
He said I would but I wouldn't count on it.

HEY, KIDS!

My doctor asked me, when is your birthday?
I told him July 12th. What year? He asked. I needed to think for a moment and told him, every year.

HEY, KIDS!

I have decided to buy Grandma a pick axe and a shovel for her next birthday. This is because she just loves digging up the past.

HEY, KIDS!

I broke a glass in the kitchen. Grandma heard it smash and called out from the other room.
Stay still, I'm coming with the broom. I told her not to rush, she can come on foot if she likes.
Does anyone have a spare room?

HEY, KIDS!
I have just written to the local council complaining about the monkey bars in our parks. Do we really want to encourage monkeys to drink in front of our children?

HEY, KIDS!
I am not happy with McDonalds. Last night on the way home I went through the drive through and ordered two large fries. What do you think I got, about 75 long skinny ones.

HEY, KIDS!
Grandma and I have decided that we need to brush our teeth together. This is because our dentist told us that brushing alone does not prevent cavities.

HEY, KIDS!
I went for a drive to the airport. I was very disappointed when I saw a sign that said Airport left. I had no choice but turn around and go home.

HEY, KIDS!
I was at this restaurant and the waiter asks me, comfortable Sir. I told him no, I had come for food.

HEY, KIDS!
I have been keeping my guitar in my car lately.

I find it great to have handy if I find myself in a traffic jam.

HEY, KIDS!
The man who invented cough mixture died last week. It probably won't surprise you but there was no coffin at his funeral.

HEY, KIDS!
My favourite teacher at school was Miss Turtle.
It's a funny name but she tortoise well.

HEY, KIDS!
Grandma was talking to me about our new neighbours. Grandma told me that whenever the husband arrives home, he gives his wife a big hug and a passionate kiss. Grandma looked and me and said, why don't you do that? I told her that I don't know her that well yet.

HEY, KIDS!
I just got a new iphone for Grandma.
That's a pretty good trade don't you think?

HEY, KIDS!
When I was at school my teacher told me that I didn't need to worry about spelling because in the future there will be this thing called auto correct.
I am very grapefruit for that teacher.

HEY, KIDS!
I asked Grandma if I could touch her hair. She said I could so I rubbed my finger over her top lip.
That's how the fight started.

HEY, KIDS!
Grandma took me out to dinner last night to a new restaurant called Kama. You won't believe it but the entire menu was just desserts.

HEY, KIDS!
I decided to write a book on snakes. In hindsight It would have been a lot easier to write it on paper.

HEY, KIDS!
I just learnt that the guy who stole my diary died. My thoughts are with his family.

HEY, KIDS!
I decided to sleep in the laundry in our dryer. It was nice and warm. The reason I chose to do this was I was hoping to wake up wrinkle free and two sizes smaller. Don't try it, it doesn't work.

HEY, KIDS!
When I was young and lived on a farm I would often go out at night on my horse. I would always take an old oil lamp so I could find my way and see where I was going. I was before my time. I was the pioneer of saddle light navigation.

HEY, KIDS!
Every morning I go for my walk and the same thing happens, I walk around the corner at the end of my street and bang, I get run into by a bike. It's becoming a vicious cycle.

HEY, KIDS!
Grandma told me that there are three women who live in our street who all got flowers delivered for Valentines Day. "They're gorgeous" Grandma said. "I know, that's why they got them."

HEY, KIDS!
When I was little and going to Kindergarten, I told my teacher that I really wanted to play the little fat boy in the Christmas play. "Do you mean the little drummer boy?" the teacher asked. I said "no, the little fat boy." "But there isn't a little fat boy in the Christmas story" the teacher said. I assured her that there was because I heard my mum singing about him.
His name is Round John Virgin.

HEY, KIDS!
The great ancient Viking warrior Rudolf the Red, so named because of the colour of his complexion, stood staring at the clear blue sky above the horizon. TODAY THERE WILL BE RAIN, he stated. His wife, who was also gazing into the clear blue sky above the horizon asked, how can you be so sure? BECAUSE RUDOLF THE RED KNOWS RAIN DEAR.

HEY, KIDS!
If you are ever thinking of getting married consider carefully if you can afford it. First you have the engagement ring, then you have the wedding ring, then you have the suffering.

HEY, KIDS!
I just saw a man crying while mowing his lawn. I asked him if he was okay?

"I'm alright," he said "I am just going through a rough patch."

HEY, KIDS!
Grandma and I went on a camping trip. We set up our tent in a nice open space. During the night Grandma woke me up and said, "look up, what do you see?" I told her that I could see millions of beautiful stars. Grandma replied, "and what do you think that means?" "It means that we are a part of a massive great, wonderful universe," I said.
Grandma rolls over and slaps me. "No, you idiot, it means that someone stole our tent."

HEY, KIDS!
I was looking through my old papers and found an old school test. I was a clever boy.

Question one. In which battle did Napoleon die?

I wrote, his last one. Ha ha.

Question two. Where was the declaration for Independence signed? I wrote, at the bottom of the page. Ha ha ha.

Question three. The Yarra River flows in which state? I wrote, liquid state. Ha ha ha ha.

Question four. What is the main reason for divorce in Australia? My answer, marriage. I kill me!

HEY, KIDS!
A termite walks into a bar and asks, is the bartender here?

HEY, KIDS!
Grandma was supervising me doing a little job. I was taking my time as I didn't want to make a mistake especially when she was watching me. Grandma said, "you are so frustrating to watch, you are just like a reluctant potato." "And what is a reluctant potato?" I asked. "A hesitater" she said.

HEY, KIDS!
Grandma and I made a pizza yesterday. It's my job to make the sauce and it's Grandma's job to do the cheese. She the gratest.

HEY, KIDS!
Grandma and I just found a suitcase in the park at the end of our street with a kangaroo and a joey in it. We rang the RSPCA who asked me,"are they moving?" I told them that I didn't know but that would explain the suitcase.

HEY, KIDS!
Grandma and I unfortunately had a little accident yesterday. We were driving our car when it happened. Then crash! We were fortunate that we only hit a lamppost and we received only light injuries.
All good.

HEY, KIDS!
I was just talking to my neighbour. He told me that his wife left him last week. She went out for milk and never came back, he said. I asked him how he was coping. All right he replied, I'm just using some of that powdered stuff.

HEY, KIDS!
Grandma saw me standing on the bathroom scales sucking in my stomach. She thought that was funny and told me that sucking in my stomach wouldn't help. I assured her that it definitely did help because it was the only way I could see the numbers.

HEY, KIDS!
Grandma just told me that I never listen to her.
At least that what I think she said.

HEY, KIDS!
Grandma is getting really inventive. She believes that she can build an invisible plane. It's a great idea but I really can't see it happening.

HEY, KIDS!
I just realized that the number seven has the word even in it. I find this to be rather odd.

HEY, KIDS!
Grandma and I went into the local bottle shop and were enquiring about a bottle of wine for old people. The nice man showed us one he believed would be ideal. He told us that it was made from an anti-diuretic hybrid grape which reduces the number of times people of our age need to go to the toilet during the night. It's called Pino More.

HEY, KIDS!
Grandma told me that midwives are really great people and deserve more recognition and credit than they get. After all, they are always helping people out.

HEY, KIDS!
I dreamt that I was wondering though a cemetery on a dark gloomy night and tripped up on a grave stone. It had my name on it. I woke up startled hoping it was only a grave mistake.

HEY, KIDS!
This kid who lives up the street was taken to hospital after swallowing 6 little plastic horses. The Doctor said that he would be okay and described his condition as stable.

HEY, KIDS!
Someone is trying to sell me a 65 inch HD TV for $10. The only thing wrong with it is the volume switch is broken. I don't think I can turn that down. What do you think?

HEY, KIDS!
I worked out the difference between a well-dressed man riding a bike and a poorly dressed man riding a unicycle. It's only attire.

HEY, KIDS!
I have been looking around at Health Insurance companies to see if I can get a better deal. I came across GMHBA. I asked them what it stands for. They asked me what I think it stands for, so I told them "Grand-Ma Has Beautiful AA-sets.

HEY, KIDS!
I have decided to do my PHD researching the impact of stomach gas on the ozone layer. If my research shows what I think it will I am going to invent a human exhaust pipe and go into business. Of course, I will need to start at the bottom.

HEY, KIDS!
I wanted to surprise Grandma by cooking her a special dinner on the last night of our holiday. I found this special recipe for a rice salad. I had a bit of trouble at first particularly when the recipe said to soak thoroughly before steaming the rice. So, I took a long bath, but Grandma seemed more surprised when I dished it up. The recipe clearly stated that it is best served without dressing.

HEY, KIDS!
The worst type of people in the world are judgemental people. I really hate them. I can recognise these people the moment I first lay eyes on them.

HEY, KIDS!
Here I am in Queensland. Grandma and I went out to dinner last night. I called the waitress over and told her that my steak was bad. She picked up my steak, turned it over, slapped it hard and put it back on my plate. She looked at me and said, if it gives you any more trouble just let me know, and she walked off.

HEY, KIDS!
Before I knew your Grandma, I went out for a short time with a girl named Loraine. That is until I met Claire Lee. Loraine was not happy and broke up with me. I remember writing a song at the time.
It went something like this.
I can see Claire Lee now Loraine is gone.

HEY, KIDS!
Grandma and I have worked hard at making our marriage work. Twice a week we go out for a nice meal and to enjoy a special night out.
Grandma goes on Wednesdays and I go on Fridays.

HEY, KIDS!
Last night I asked Grandma why we always argue about everything. She said that she can never agree with me because we can't afford both to be wrong.

HEY, KIDS!
You should see my damaged luggage after we arrived home from Queensland. It was so damaged that I decided to take it and show it to my lawyer.
The lawyer took one look at it and said 'you don't have much of a case". I said I know, that's why I'm here.

HEY, KIDS!
A brunette, a blonde and a dedhead decide to donate blood. So off they went to the blood bank.
When they arrived, they were each given a form to fill in. The brunette listed her blood type as B positive. The blonde listed her blood type as B negative. The dedhead looked at her form and said, I think I'm a typo.

HEY, KIDS!
Grandma and I just had a new security door installed.
The only problem with it is every time I touch the
handle it gives off a static electric shock. I contacted
the company and can you guess what they said?
They said that they would make me another door free
of charge. Funny, funny people. I was shocked.

HEY, KIDS!
Since I have been diagnosed with diabetes I have been
doing a lot of reading about healthy eating.
I just read an article that said that most people eat
more scraps and junk food than dogs.
Hello, I can't even remember that last time I ate a dog.

HEY, KIDS!
I had an appointment with a psychic for next week.
You won't believe this, but she just rang and told me
that I wouldn't be able to make it.

HEY, KIDS!
Don't you just love the word gullible.
Upside down it looks like a crocodile.

HEY, KIDS!
Today Grandma and I are going to pick up
our new glasses. After that we'll see.

HEY, KIDS!
Grandma came out this morning and said, hey Grandad
do you want to hear a construction joke? Of course,
I said. I can't, she replied, because I'm still working on
it. She now thinks she's the funny one.

HEY, KIDS!
Does anybody remember the dog that we had many years ago? We called him Isaiah. We called him that because when you looked at him closely you could see that one eye was higher than the other.

HEY, KIDS!
Grandma and I just went out for morning tea. Now that I am diabetic, I have to watch what I eat. I was looking at the cakes and asked the server, is this gluten free? He looked at me and said, no, it's $4.50.

HEY, KIDS!
It's our anniversary today. Grandma and I have been looking back over the last 48 years. She just said, you know, at first I didn't know what you and I had in common. I told her that it was obvious, they are both vowels. Not so happy anniversary anymore.

HEY, KIDS!
Our local council is extremely strict. A dog gave birth to five puppies recently in a local park and was fined for littering.

HEY, KIDS!
When I use my BBQ now, I like to use small pieces of asteroid instead of beef. I still like beef but I believe that the asteroids are just a little meteor.

HEY, KIDS!
My Granddaughter just said, "I hope you are going to shave off that Moustache before we go on our holiday, it's embarrassing". I was impressed. That's the bravest things that I have ever heard anyone say to Grandma.

HEY, KIDS!
When I was in Queensland, I showed Grandma a pen that could write under water. Grandma seemed impressed until I told her that it could write other words too.

HEY, KIDS!
I still have my good looks and charm. It's true. Yesterday at the airport five women asked me to go out. Unfortunately, it was because I had gone into the wrong bathroom.

HEY, KIDS!
I can remember when I was young playing in the backyard with my little brother after it had rained. We had some holes in the yard that always filled with water. I can remember that I grabbed my brother's head and pushed it into one of the holes under the water. My mum saw what I was doing through the window and came running out to rescue my brother. Why on earth would you do that to your brother she yelled. I explained that that we were playing church and that I was baptising him. In the name of the Father, the Son, and in the hole he goes.

HEY, KIDS!
During check in on our flight to Queensland a staff member apologised and told me that I would be in seat 48B and Grandma would be in seat 88B. I jokingly thanked her and asked her if I needed to pay any extra for the privilege.
She said no, Grandma had already paid.

HEY, KIDS!
You all know that I have been working hard to overcome my hiking addiction. Well, I am just letting you know that I am doing well, but I'm not out of the woods yet.

HEY, KIDS!
I am sending today's joke from my hospital bed. Grandma and I were out digging holes to plant some trees yesterday when a bee stung me on my forehead. Grandma tells me that I was fortunate that she was close enough to squash it with her shovel.

HEY, KIDS!
You know that vets are very expensive don't you. My pet frog looked sick so I rushed him to the vet. By the time we got there he wasn't moving. The Vet examined him and said he was dead. I couldn't accept this so I begged the Vet to do everything he could to be sure. The Vet left the room and came back with a black Labrador dog. The dog sniffed the frog, sat down and looked at me with very sad eyes. The Vet left the room again and came back with a cat. The cat circled the frog a few times and walked out of the room. The Vet then told me that my frog was definitely dead and there was nothing more anyone could do. He then handed me a bill for $1000. What, $1000 just to tell me that my frog is dead. He explained that it would have only cost $100 if I didn't insist on the lab report and the cat scan which were $450 each.

HEY, KIDS!
Grandma cooked fresh fish last night. I didn't like it and I told her it was dry. She said, hey that maybe because it had been taken out of the water.
She is getting funnier by the day.

HEY, KIDS!
Yesterday I was driving to the supermarket and stopped at the lights. A couple of car jackers jumped in the car, threw me out and stole everything, including my car.
I think they were "Pirates of the Car I Be In".

HEY, KIDS!
I have come up with another great idea.
I reckon that I can make a thought-controlled body
deodorant. Grandma thinks it a ridiculous idea,
but I told her that it makes scents
when you think about it.

HEY, KIDS!
I asked Grandma "what does the yellow light on the
traffic signal mean"? She said "slow down". I said
O K A Y, W H A T   D O E S   T H E   Y E L L
O W   L I G H T O N   T H E
T R A F F I C   S I G N A L
M - E - A - NNNNNNNNNNNN?   She hit me.

HEY, KIDS!
Grandma and I went scuba diving when we were on
our holidays. It was great and we had a great instructor.
He was very helpful. I asked him why scuba divers
always sit on the side of the boat and
fall backwards into the water.
He told me, "it's because if they fall forwards they
would still be in the boat".

HEY, KIDS!
When we were on holidays, we saw a lot of people
walking dogs. One lady was walking two dogs.
Grandma asked her if they were Jack Russell's.
They lady replied rather meanly and said,
"no, they're mine".

HEY, KIDS!
Last night Grandma told me that what we need is some
cold, hard cash. So, when she went to bed,
I put her purse in the frezzer.

HEY, KIDS!
I remember the one year I forgot our anniversary. When I arrived home Grandma seemed to be in a bit of a mood. After awhile she asked me how I would feel if I didn't see her for a while. Because I was sensing her mood, I told her that would be okay.
I didn't see her Friday, I didn't see her Saturday, I didn't see her Sunday, I didn't see her Monday but by Tuesday the swelling had started to go down and I could see her again. Never forget an anniversary.

HEY, KIDS!
When I was away, I went into the toilets off the foyer in the Hotel we were staying. There was a big sign on the wall that said, EMPLOYEES MUST WASH HANDS. I waited for over an hour and no one came to wash mine, so I gave the place a negative review.

HEY, KIDS!
Our backyard has just been invaded by millions of flesh-eating flying insects. We need help. Someone, please call the SWAT team.

HEY, KIDS!
Before we got married Grandma had two men chasing her, me and this handsome young doctor.
Every day the doctor would give your Grandma a red rose.
Not to be outdone, everyday I would give your Grandma an apple. Your Grandma seemed to be confused with my gifts and after some time asked me what was the meaning of all the apples.
I told her that my mother had taught me, an apple a day keeps the doctor away.
I won.

HEY, KIDS!
Grandma has not been very well. I took her to the doctor. The doctor wrote her a prescription for antibiotics. We had the prescription made up at the Pharmacy. On the bottle the instructions said, TAKE ONE TABLET 3 TIMES A DAY. Grandma and I were fine taking it the first time but neither of us can figure out a way to get it back up. Even Google couldn't help.

HEY, KIDS!
Grandma and I went out for breakfast. They were offering a senior's special of bacon and eggs, hash brown, pancakes and a coffee for just $10.00. Grandma said that she would have the special without the eggs. The waitress told her that she could not change the specials offer and if she wanted everything else without the eggs it would cost her $21.00. Grandma told her that she would have the special. How would like your eggs done? the waitress asked. Raw, hard in the shell, in a bag to go, Grandma told her. Grandma brought the eggs home and made me a cake. Smart woman your Grandma.

HEY, KIDS!
Yesterday Grandma and I were working in the garden again. I was practicing my jokes on her when she threw a bag of fertiliser all over me. I thought she was inferring that my jokes stink, but she made it clear it was an effort to make me grow up.

HEY, KIDS!
I bumped into one of my Granddaughters out shopping yesterday. She said that she was out shopping for her dad. This confused me a bit because I thought she was happy with the one she had.

HEY, KIDS!
I told Grandma that I would take her to the Elvis Steak House. She said that she had never heard of the Elvis Steak House. Of course, you have, I told her.
It's the place where people love meat tender.

HEY, KIDS!
Grandma and I once lived next door to a neighbour who had a dog that barked constantly. One Saturday morning when we were trying to sleep in, the dog barked and barked and barked. Grandma said, that's enough. She got up and left the room. She was only gone a few minutes before she came back.
What did you do? I asked her, the dog is still barking. Grandma said, I put the dog in our back
yard to see how they like it.

HEY, KIDS!
I once had a friend who had a bad stutter. I called him Donkey. I introduced him to your Grandma once.
She asked him, why does he call you Donkey?
He answered, he aw, he aw,
he aw, he always calls me that.

HEY, KIDS!
Grandma ordered some new blinds for our bedroom. Two very nice men just came and installed them.
Kurt and Rod.

HEY, KIDS!
There is a story in the Bible that talks about Lot's wife. The story says she looked back and turned into a pillar of salt. I don't think that is anything really special.
Your Grandma looked back once while driving the car and turned into a telephone pole.

HEY, KIDS!
I was talking to Grandma because she seemed rather confused. It turns out she was trying to figure out why she has only two sisters and her brother has three.

HEY, KIDS!
Before Grandma and I got married I had to ask her dad for permission. He asked me,
have you seen her mother?
I replied, yes Sir, but I still prefer your daughter.

HEY, KIDS!
A few years ago I accidentally cut the dog's tail off with the whipper snipper. Grandma wrapped the dog in a towel and jumped in the car. Where are you going? I asked. Grandma told me she was going to KMART. Why are you taking the dog to to KMART? Because KMART is one of the biggest retailers in the world.

HEY, KIDS!
I can always get myself in trouble. The other night at my grandson's birthday party two big women walked in and ordered some drinks from the bar. I couldn't help but notice their distinctive accent. Are you two ladies from Ireland? I asked. They weren't very friendly and snapped back at me. It's Wales you idiot.
I couldn't help myself and said, okay, are you two whales from Ireland? I'm in ward three, second floor.

HEY, KIDS!
The people of the world are starting to feel guilty and concerned about the amount of junk and waste we are leaving in space.
The next spacecraft that is being launched is going to be called Apolo G.

HEY, KIDS!
I bought a lizard from the local pet shop. Lizards are supposed to be quiet relaxing pets to have. However, my lizard never shut up. It just kept telling dad jokes all day long. In the end I had had enough and took it back to the pet shop. The bloke there took one look at my lizard and said, that's not a lizard, it's a stand-up chameleon.

HEY, KIDS!
Did you know that Grandma is in her seventies and still doesn't need glasses. That's right, she drinks straight out of the bottle.

HEY, KIDS!
I can remember when I was little finding the old family Bible. I opened it and found an old leaf pressed between the pages. My mum walked in and asked, what have you found there? I replied, I'm not sure but I think it's Adam's suit.

HEY, KIDS!
I've got something that I feel I need to say to you all. And if I am going to be frank, I am going to have to change my name.

HEY, KIDS!
I feel the need to encourage you today. I want to say, don't worry about making mistakes. I was taught that you learn from your mistakes. I've learnt so much that I have decided to make some more.

HEY, KIDS!
We have been babysitting again. Grandma just said to me, this baby has been crying for two hours non-stop, can you please take over for a while? I said sure, but now I'm starting to get a sore throat and red eyes.

HEY, KIDS!
Do you remember the time when Grandma got stung by a jellyfish? It was quite funny really. Grandma yelled at me, quick pee on it. So I ran into the water and found that darn jellyfish and said, that's for stinging my wife.

HEY, KIDS!
Me and a workmate were given the task of measuring the height of this very big flagpole. We tried a lot of ladders but none of them even came close to being big enough. Then this know-it-all bloke comes along and asks what we are doing. We told him that we needed to get the height of the flagpole. The smart know-it-all bloke pulls out a wrench, undoes the bolts on the bottom, lays the pole down, runs a long tape from one end to the other, writes the measurement on a piece of paper, gives it to us and walks off. I looked at my mate and said, now he wasn't very smart was he, we told him that we needed the height and he gives us the width.

HEY, KIDS!
I woke up this morning with a serious vision problem. I can't see myself doing much today.

HEY, KIDS!
I can remember going to church when I was younger and getting all excited about this Olly Looya guy.

I never saw him and I think that he may have been lost or just hiding somewhere because everyone kept calling out his name very loudly over and over again.

HEY, KIDS!

When I was a teenager and went on my first blind date. I was so excited and I didn't quite know what to expect. My friend, who arranged the date told me that there was something that I should know. He told me that she was expecting a baby. So, what I did was put on a bonnet and a nappy and waited in the coffee shop.
I was such an idiot.

HEY, KIDS!

Now that I am diabetic my doctor told me that I need to keep an eye on my feet. If I lose feeling in my feet or my toes start to go black I have to go to the hospital immediately.
I thought great, now I am black toes intolerant as well.

HEY, KIDS!

I just found out that someone wrote a book about the old outside dunnies we had when I was a kid.
If you are interested in an good read it's called,
Fifty Metres to the Outhouse by Willy Makit.
The Illustrations have been done by Betty Wont.

HEY, KIDS!

This man I know started his own landscaping business. He employed 3 men to help him on his first job. One was an Australian, one was a Scotsman and one was Chinese. He met them on site and gave them their jobs. He told the Australian guy that he wanted him to mix some concrete and start on a concrete path. He told the Scotsman that he wanted him to shovel and spread a big pile of soil. Then he told the Chinese man that he was in charge of supplies and to keep the others up with the supplies they needed. The boss left to pick up some other things he needed. When the boss returned, he found only 2 men standing around and no work had been done. He said to the Australian, I thought I told you to make a concrete path.

Sorry mate, with no concrete and no mixer, crickey what do you think a bloke can do? You put that little Chinese fella in charge of supplies and I haven't laid eyes on him since ya left. The boss turned to the Scotsman and said, what about you? I thought I told you to spread this pile of soil. Aye ye did laddie said the Scotsman, but I couldnea get maself a shoovel.
Ye left the wee Chinese laddie in charge of supplies and I havna seen im since ya left. The three men walked over to the house and from behind the big pile of sand the Chinese man jumped up and shouted "SUPPLIES".

HEY, KIDS!
Did I ever tell you that I went out with a crossed eyed girl. It didn't work out. We could never see eye to eye on anything and I always thought she was seeing someone else on the side.

HEY, KIDS!
You know the older I get the more I think about the people that I have lost over the years.
When I reflect on my past I realize now that I never should have taken on that job as a tour guide.

HEY, KIDS!
Grandma always tries to draw me into her boring conversations with her friends. Which hand is the correct hand to stir your tea with? Who cares? Grandma says she thinks it's the left hand, her friend Matalida insists it's the right hand. Which hand to you use Grandad? Neither, I use a spoon.

HEY, KIDS!
Grandma and I went a saw a new movie. It was about a pig with no eye. Yep, it was rated PG.

HEY, KIDS!
We were minding our youngest granddaughter today and she asked, Grandad, can you make a noise like a frog? Croak, croak, croak, I said. Thank you, now I'm going on a holiday to Disney Land. Why is that? I asked. Because my dad told me that once you croak it, he will take me there.

HEY, KIDS!
I saw this old bloke walking through the shopping centre with two massive frozen chips, one under each arm. I stopped him and asked why he was using two massive frozen chips as walking sticks.
He said, they're McCains.

HEY, KIDS!
I just found out that my uncle was a mime.
I never knew. He never talked about it.

HEY, KIDS!
I am writing this from my hospital bed again. I'm okay, nothing really to worry about. Yesterday Grandma was trying to help me with a small job outside banging in some stakes. Grandma would not hold the stakes so I had to do it.
Then Grandma didn't know how to use the hammer. I told her that I would hold the stake and when I nod my head you hit it.
I nodded my head and the next thing I know I'm in here.

HEY, KIDS!
Grandma just visited me at the hospital.
She tried to explain what happened yesterday. She said that she couldn't help it because the stakes were too high.

HEY, KIDS!
Grandma and I were at the supermarket looking at the meat. I found a twin pack of venison burgers but Grandma said that I couldn't buy them because they were two deer.

HEY, KIDS!
I have decided to take up a new hobby. I am going to start collecting coins. Grandma says that the change will do me good.

HEY, KIDS!
The ambulance that was seen coming into our estate this morning was not for us. It was just for me. Grandma and I decided to have another go at putting in the stakes. I made sure that they were not too high this time but things turned out just the same.
I'm back at the hospital. I'm starting to think that it might be something I said.

HEY, KIDS!
I made fish tacos today and I learnt something new. I learn that fish are ungrateful creatures. Yep, they just swam away without even trying them.

HEY, KIDS!
I just learned that someone is stabbed every 52 seconds in Australia. I don't believe it. I don't believe it because surely, they would be dead by now.

HEY, KIDS!
Never tell your Grandma that her nylon stockings are wrinkled unless you are 100% sure she is wearing them. I always seem to learn the hard way.

HEY, KIDS!
I just heard that Kerry Packer's son has a bit of a reputation around town. He has been described as an animal. Be careful if you need to do business with Al.

HEY, KIDS!
Grandma says that it is time that I got myself a part time job. I told her that there are no jobs for a 70 year old retired worn out old man. Yes there are, she told me, you can apply to join the search and rescue squad, they are always looking for someone.

HEY, KIDS!
Today I bought a 12 year old whisky. Grandma told me that it was a big mistake and his mother wasn't very happy either.

HEY, KIDS!
Yesterday I walked into a Hotel carrying my new set of jumper leads. The bouncer stopped me and wouldn't let me in. Of course, I asked why?
He told me that it looks to him like that I have come to try and start something.

HEY, KIDS!
A funny thing happened yesterday. Grandma and I went to this new Chinese restaurant for lunch. The owner came out and was very friendly. In general conversation he asked me, "what you like do?"

I had to think a bit and in the end I told him I like to tell jokes. He thought this was great, ha, ha ha. "Yoo lake me wauff, you lake me wauff. Yoo say funny yoke and lake me wauff. Yoo lake me wauff and yoo no pay, flood flee for yoo, yoo no pay, all flee. I tried to think of one of my jokes and as I was thinking I noticed behind him big flames jumping out of this massive wok in the kitchen. I panicked a bit and shouted wok, wok.

Ha, ha, whose dare? He said. I said no, no, wok, wok. He said Wok who? I couldn't resit it any more so I said, wok and wole. Ha, ha, yoo have flee lunch.

HEY, KIDS!
A word of elderly wisdom. If you are ever trying to escape a taxidermist, never play dead.

HEY, KIDS!
Last night Grandma and I went out for dinner. I was so hungry that I ordered this big juicy steak. I told Grandma that Budapest was going to love it.
What are you talking about she said, who is Budapest?
Budapest is my stomach I told her.
Why have you named your stomach Budapest?
Because Budapest is the capital of Hungary.

HEY, KIDS!
I just heard this clutter from the laundry. So, I went to investigate and I found Grandma trying to put bricks under the front of the washing machine.
What are you doing? I asked. Grandma told me that she has just been reading the old washing machine manual and it told her that the machine washes best at 30 degrees.

HEY, KIDS!
Did I ever tell you that before I decided to marry your Grandma, she told me that she was interesting and I believed her. This was the main reason I married her. Unfortunately, after we were married, she changed her story and denied ever saying it.
She tells me that what she really said was, that she was in to resting, and she loves her sleep.

HEY, KIDS!
I decided to do some community work and join a
support group to work with kleptomaniacs.
Most of them only attended because of court orders.
Unfortunately, I was running a bit late for our first
meeting and when I got there all the seats were taken.

HEY, KIDS!
Grandma and I were on the train and this little girl was
making faces at Grandma. Typical Grandma couldn't
resist trying to teach the young girl a lesson.
Grandma said to her, my mother taught me that if I
pulled ugly faces like that and the wind changed then I
would stay that way.
The young girl replied, well you can't
say you weren't warned.

HEY, KIDS!
I wanted to get something for Grandma for her
birthday. I bought her a new bracelet.
I don't think she likes it because she asked me
"why does it say do not resuscitate?"

HEY, KIDS!
Grandma came out this morning and said.
Hey Grandad, if that is a suppository in your ear,
where is your hearing aid?

HEY, KIDS!
Grandma has had trouble sleeping.
At 2 o'clock this morning I told her that she
has to stop bringing her problems to bed.
She said, where are you going to sleep then?

HEY, KIDS!
I had to speak to Grandma about being mean. I asked her if she had been telling people that I was an idiot. She said that she was sorry and didn't realise that it was a secret.

HEY, KIDS!
There is a first time for everything. Yesterday I washed the car with Grandma. Our neighbour came over and asked me why I just didn't use a sponge.

HEY, KIDS!
Yesterday I asked Grandma if she would help me with the Barbeque for today. This morning I couldn't find her anywhere. I rang her phone and she told me that she was still waiting in line at the toy store.

HEY, KIDS!
I am so proud that all of you are so bright and intelligent. Do you ever wonder where you get all this intelligence from? It must be your Grandma because I still have all of mine.

HEY, KIDS!
Grandma said to me, hey Grandad, let's go out and have some fun tonight. I said OKAY, but if you get home before me, leave the front light on.

HEY, KIDS!
Grandma asked me what I would like for Christmas this year. I told her a wheelchair. What do you want a wheelchair for, she asked? So, I told her. It's because she likes to push me around and talk behind my back.

HEY, KIDS!
I went to the doctor because I was feeling confused
and a bit delusional. I told him that I woke up this
morning thinking that I was a deck of cards.
He told me to sit and wait in the waiting room
and that he would deal with me in a minute.

HEY, KIDS!
Before we got married Grandma told me that after we
were married, she wanted to share all my worries and
problems. I told her that I didn't have any worries or
problems. She said, I know, but we are not married yet.

HEY, KIDS!
Agent 86 Maxwell Smart went undercover working as a
school teacher. He chose the name Mr Bydat-Much.

HEY, KIDS!
Grandma asked me if I could remember the stupidest
thing that I have ever said. I do.

HEY, KIDS!
I was sitting on the train looking at this man opposite
me who I thought looked strangely familiar. He looked
at me and asked, why are you looking at me?
I said, I'm sorry it's just that you look just like my wife,
except for the beard.
But I don't have a beard, he said.
I know but my wife does.

HEY, KIDS!
I have a question for all you mind readers out there?

HEY, KIDS!
I have been researching British history. I discovered that there once was a Knight who could not go into battle because when he did, he would always break a bone. He was considered very fragile.
His name was Sir Ramic. Apparently,
he was one of the Knights of the kitchen table.

HEY, KIDS!
Lee Wong and Su Wong fell in love and got married. When their first child was born, he was white and didn't look Chinese at all.
The nurse at the hospital asked them what they were going to name the baby? Lee and Su were very confused as they pondered what to call their son. Lee said, this proves that 2 Wongs can make a White. So, they called the
baby Sum Tim Wong.

HEY, KIDS!
Grandma is wanting to save money and won't let me turn the heater on. I get very cold. Last night when I said that I was cold, she took my chair and put in in the corner and told me to sit there. I asked why? Grandma said that the corner is the warmest
place in the room. It's 90 degrees.

HEY, KIDS!
Did you know that every year Neil Diamond would go to Sweden and sing Christmas carols with the locals. He would get them to stand in a line right along the main street and everyone would sing.
It was Sweet Carol Line.

HEY, KIDS!
When Grandma and I were in Egypt we went to a souvenir shop and tried to buy a glific. They wouldn't sell us one. So, we went to another souvenir shop and they wouldn't sell us one either. No matter where we went no-one would sell us a glific.
Apparently, you can only a hire a glific in Egypt.

HEY, KIDS!
I was thinking back to my first job. I was working as a jump lead tester. It wasn't much of a job but what the heck, I had to start somewhere.

HEY, KIDS!
You should never trust a soldier. I rented a house to one once who listed his rank as Captain. He didn't pay any rent for 6 weeks so I went around to see him. He was gone, left without a trace. It was then that I realized that he had lied. He wasn't a Captain at all, he was just a left tenant.

HEY, KIDS!
My new car has a button for almost everything. There is even a button that says "Rear Wiper".
I am too scared to push that one.

HEY, KIDS!
I was wondering how many of us would be in favour of bringing Roman Numerals back into fashion? I for one.

HEY, KIDS!
I once had a job for a short time on a dairy farm. I didn't work there very long, they said that I had to leave because I was a danger to myself and udders.

HEY, KIDS!
My detective instincts have been kicking in again. I have been suspecting that someone has been dumping soil in my garden, bit by bit. I have been keeping a lookout but I haven't seen anyone so far.
However, the plot continues to thicken.

HEY, KIDS!
More soil dumped in my garden today. The plot is getting deeper. I'm starting to think that someone close to me might be a plant.

HEY, KIDS!
Today I tried to make some cool aid. I wish these companies would get the instructions right. There was no way I could get 8 glasses of water into that little packet.

HEY, KIDS!
Grandma and I went to the funeral of our friend Dave the chicken. We may never know why the chicken crossed the road, but what we do know is, he is now on the other side.

HEY, KIDS!
You won't believe this but yesterday Grandma bought a new scarf. This morning she decided to take it back because she says it's too tight.

HEY, KIDS!
Grandma and I have decided to try waterskiing. Unfortunately, so far we haven't been able to find a river or lake with enough slope.

HEY, KIDS!
I can remember a nickname my workmates gave me many years ago. They called me "Batteries". I think this was because I was never included in anything.

HEY, KIDS!
Grandma and I cooked some bear meat hamburgers last night. I don't recommend them, too grizzly.

HEY, KIDS!
Grandma told me why actors always say "break a leg" before they go on stage. She reckons it's because they just love being in a cast.

HEY, KIDS!
Did you know that I really love going out doors. I find it much easier than going out the windows.

HEY, KIDS!
I have ordered a new axe all the way from Italy. They just notified me that it has been posted and it's on the way. Okay, I can now truthfully say that I have a foreign axe sent.

HEY, KIDS!
One of my mates told me to leave my car at the pub and take the bus home. According to the policeman I was in no fit state to drive that home either.

HEY, KIDS!
Grandma got all excited because I signed up for an exercise program that requires me to walk 5 kilometres every day. I asked her why she was so happy about it. She said, because in one week you will be 35 kilometres further away.

HEY, KIDS!
My credit card was rejected at the clothing store while I was trying to buy a new jumper. They looked and me and told me to try the cardigan.
No way.

HEY, KIDS!
Grandma and I visited the cemetery yesterday. As we were standing there looking over all the graves, Grandma stood there pondering for a moment. I wonder what all these people would be doing now if they were still alive? She said. I told her that they would probably be knocking loudly on the lid and shouting "let me out".

HEY, KIDS!
Did I ever tell you that I used to live next door to a girl with a wooden leg named Mavis.
I don't remember the name of her other leg.

HEY, KIDS!
Yesterday someone knocked on my front door. I wasn't expecting anyone and I am not comfortable opening the door to strangers, so I called out "who's there?" This strange voice answered, "Didja".
I don't know anyone named Didja so I asked, Didja who? Didja hear me knocking? Then he said, "Eleva wants to ask you a question. "Eleva who? Eleva Nuisance. Then he left.

HEY, KIDS!
I have been away for over a week helping a friend to look after a sick cow. I told Grandma that I won't be able to come home until it gets better.
She seems to think I am milking it.

HEY, KIDS!
Grandma and I met some new neighbours today who are of American Indian heritage. He introduced himself as Tonto and he introduced his wife as Four Horses. We were surprised at her name but tried to be respectful of their culture. I asked him if it was a common name in their culture? No he said,
Four Horses mean nag, nag, nag, nag.

HEY, KIDS!
I just love Christmas. I love sitting and looking at all the presents under the tree. Somehow, I always know what is wrapped up inside each parcel. It's a gift.

HEY, KIDS!
Do you know why the Queen could never be found guilty of anything? It's because she was in a cent.

HEY, KIDS!
Grandma and I have another new Irish neighbour. I asked him how he liked Australia. He said, too many flies, the Gooverment is terrible, the food here is no good, the weader is atrocious, it's eider too hot or too cold. Us Irish need to take over this country and show you people how to do tings right.
My name is Phil. Phil O'Stein.
You remember dat name. Me and my udder friend Phil, Phil O'Sophical are going to stand for goovernment and be the prime Minister.